The Altars Will
Alter Your Life Forever

Shirley Nash

xulon
PRESS

DEDICATION

This book is dedicate to my beloved grandchildren
Zakia, Reginald III, Jihaad, Shanice,
Cianni, Diequan, Kayla, Maniyah and Ashley;
along with all future generations to come.

Life is God, and God is Life.

My prayer is for you to know Him in all His Glory.

TABLE OF CONTENTS

ACKNOWLEDGMENTS

I like to thank God, for my grandmother who had a prayer altar and visited it day and night to travail for the generations of our family souls and heritage. I know I stand in this place due to her endless prayers. I also thank my parents, my sister and brothers, along with a very special aunt N. Turner, who opened up the door for my salvation, and uncle Elder A. S. Paige whose educational and religious lifestyle taught me to excel in my studies.

This book was inspired from a bible class I attend with my thoughtful sister, Rochelle Henderson while studying the Old Testament. We notice how the Prophet Elijah visited the altars continuously while seeking Gods wisdom and guidance for his life. As we started to apply the lessons from the Old Testament, a pattern emerged. Therefore, I recognized the need to record this information systematically to share with others. I thank God for my sister she is my sounding board.

I thank my patient and loving husband a wonderful man of God, Elder Reginald Nash Sr. who supported my endeavors to write this book. I thank each of my children Reginald Jr., Regina, Eric and Christene for there constant encouragement, admiration in addition, respect towards me. I thank my grandchildren for further inspiration. I felt I needed to leave them, and all generations afterwards, with clear guidelines how to love, seek and serve God.

I saw the need for this book while teaching at a yearly prayer retreat under the direction of Mother M. Pew, an awesome woman of God. Each year God gave me further insight of these altars. I would share this teaching with the group until finally a book emerged.

I also thank my cousin Minister M. Fulton for helping me to arrive at the next level to publish this book. I also would like to thank the many Christian family members and pastors who poured spiritual wisdom and knowledge into my life.

INTRODUCTION

The purpose of this book is to make you aware of God's standards when we come into relationship with Him. I will attempt to show that there are altars that God has set up and altars that the devil has set up. The God ordained altars will call forth life while the Baal altars will bring death into your life. *John 10:10, The thief (devil) cometh, but for to steal, and to kill, and to destroy: Jesus stated, "I am come that they might have life, and that they might have it more abundantly."* Read Job 1:9; Mark 4:37-39; Revelation 20:2.

Each altar is based upon faith (belief) and trust (confidence) in a supernatural being. There are three entities found at these altars, God, mankind and the Devil.

At the God altars, the triune Godhead is the entity and power with which we must contend. *Isaiah 64:8…O*

LORD, thou art our father; we are the clay, and thou our potter; and we all are the work of thy hand. Acts 10:38...God anointed Jesus of Nazareth with the Holy Ghost and with power: who went about doing good, and healing all that were oppressed of the devil; for God was with him. Once you are born, you are a continual work in process. The goal is to become more like God daily which will prepare you to return home with Him. However, until then we are to work the works of Him who sent Him. We are to shed our love abroad calling all men into repentance and healing in Christ.

Mankind: It is here at these altars man is searching for the **purpose of his life**. He asks, "Why do I exist"? In man's search for the answer to this question, he will choose who will teach him his reason for being. God created man with a freewill so He gave man the power of choice. We are not robots; therefore it is man's decision to choose whom he will obey. *For to be carnally minded is death; but to be spiritually minded is life and peace* (Rom. 8:6). It is here you will learn what are your convictions based upon. At these altars, man has the potential to become a part of good or evil power. The Apostle Paul said to man in *Romans 6:16, Know ye not,* *that to whom ye yield yourselves servants to obey, his servants ye are to whom ye obey; whether of sin unto death, or of obedience unto righteousness?*

At the Baal altar, the Devil is an evil entity with whom we must contend. He was a powerful and beautiful archangel (the highest order of angels) who once abided in heaven. The Devil wanted to become equal with God, therefore <u>he chose</u> to rebel against Him and was kicked out of heaven (Isaiah 14:12). His pride was his downfall; he was not content with who he was and what he had. In Ezekiel 28:12-19, this text applies to a supernatural being (the Devil) and here you will see the five foolish prideful I will statements of the Devil. *Son of man, take up a lamentation upon the king of Tyrus, and say unto him, Thus saith the Lord God; Thou sealest up the sum, full of wisdom, and perfect in beauty. v. 13, Thou hast been in Eden the garden of God; every precious stone was thy covering, the sardius, topaz, and the diamond, the beryl, the onyx, and the jasper, the sapphire, the emerald, and the carbuncle, and gold: the workmanship of thy tabrets and of thy pipes was prepared in thee in the day that thou wast created. v. 14, Thou art the anointed cherub that covereth; and I have set thee so: thou wast upon the holy mountain of God; thou hast walked up and down in the midst of the stones of fire. v. 15, Thou wast perfect in thy ways from the day that thou wast created, till iniquity was found in thee. v. 16, By the multitude of thy merchandise they have filled the midst of thee with violence, and thou hast sinned: therefore I will cast thee as profane out of the mountain of God: and I will destroy thee, O covering cherub, from the midst of the stones of fire. v. 17, Thine heart was lifted up because of thy beauty, thou hast corrupted thy wisdom by reason of thy brightness: I will cast thee to the ground, I will lay thee before kings, that they may behold thee. v. 18, Thou hast defiled thy sanctuaries by the multitude of thine iniquities, by the iniquity of thy traffic; therefore will I bring forth a fire from the midst of thee, it shall devour thee, and I will bring thee to ashes upon the earth in the sight of all them that behold thee.* The devil desire is to trick you to become foolish like Him, reject God and His desires for your life. He wants you to say I will to him.

God altars are true altars upon where we come into relationship with our heavenly Father. These are genuine, pure and holy altars upon which we commune with the triune Godhead. The triune Godhead encompasses God, Jesus Christ and the Holy Spirit. Baal altars are impure, unholy false altars upon which a human being comes into relationship with the Devil. The Devil's trinity is the false prophet, the beast and the Antichrist. There are two kinds of altars, God's altars and Baal's altars. This book will establish four altars existing under each of the two categories.

Here are the four God altars and the relationship established at them.

1ˢᵗ Altar Faith in God, relationship of fellowship is established. You enter into a personal relationship with God. You become a new creature in Him. The old nature is crucified with Christ and a rebirth and a new nature emerges. You are saved at this altar.

2ⁿᵈ Altar Confession of Faith, relationship of sanctification is established. You enter into a relationship of cleanliness with God. The outer man (flesh) is brought under subjection through sanctification (cleansing and setting apart to become holy). The spiritual man enters into a higher relationship with Christ by obeying and surrendering to His Word (the Bible). You are sanctified at this altar.

3rd Altar Declaration of Faith, relationship of righteousness is established. The heart is circumcised (cutting out) of all unrighteousness (purged of all evil) and filled with love and forgiveness. This circumcision establishes a deeper relationship through Christ's death, burial and resurrection. It enters into a new covenant with God, which permit the Holy Spirit to dwell in you. It brings you out of reproach and into redemption. You are Holy Ghost filled at this altar and empowered for service (work for God).

4th Altar Revelation of Faith, relationship of glory is established. The believer's whole being (body soul and spirit) is unified by fire into a perfect union with God. His mind, heart, and flesh are sold completely out to God. His will, desires and motives all align with the desires of the Father (God). He does whatever God tells him to do with great joy; therefore, God shows up mightily on the believer's behalf. It is at this altar you are fired-baptized.

Here are the four Baal altars and the relationship established.

1st Baal Altar Subtle Mind Control, relationship of disobedience is established. It is at this altar the devil subtly seduces the mind of an individual. His desire is to make humanity disobey God, His Word and plan for their life.

2nd Baal Altar Subtle Body Control, relationship of rebellion is established. At this altar, he furthers his control by bringing an imbalance with the spiritual and carnal man. He tempts and leads humanity into rebellion so they will do unhealthy and vile behaviors with their flesh.

3rd Baal Altar Renders the Heart Evil, relationship of deception is established. As the altars continue, the devil deceives the person to think there is no hope for this sinful heart. He brings humanity into complaining and justifying their actions, drawing them farther down a road of sin, guilt and shame.

4th Baal Altar Denunciation of God, relationship of death. This altar declares two things to humanity lawlessness and the anti-Christ. It teachers everyone to reject and rebel against God and His biblical truths and doctrines until the conscious mind is seared. It totally denies the deity of Christ. The ultimate goal of this final Baal altar is to sentence the believer's soul to hell forever.

The God altars will lead you into a pathway of righteousness and holiness while the Baal altars will lead you down a pathway of sin and desecration. This book will tell you the purposes, motives and directives of each altar. It will show you how to apply the godly principles of each altar to your life, so you may mature in God. It will also give you guidelines to resist the pitfalls of the Baal altars. If you apply these rules to your life, they will transform you forever.

Today you have a choice to make at these altars. I hope you will choose the altar life and not death. I challenge you to seek the true and living, Holy God. It is only He who can change you. Psalm 34:8 states, "O taste and see that the Lord is good: blessed is the man that trusteth in Him."

A
L
ALTER
A
R

<u>A TRUE ALTAR WILL</u>
<u>ALTER YOUR LIFE FOREVER!</u>

We will attempt to examine and answer these questions: What is an altar? What is the purpose of an altar? Why do we need an altar? Who should build an altar? Where an altar should be built? What can we do at the altar?

What is an altar?

The word altar (from Lat. altus, "high"; ara, "elevation"; Heb. mizbeah; Gk. thusiasterion, "place of sacrifice"). The word altar is an elevated place of sacrifice, a slaughter place. In the Old Testament, the sacrifice was an animal, but in the New Testament, Jesus Christ became the sacrifice that was used for the propitiation of all humanity's sin. It (altar) was a simple elevation made of earth, rough stones or turf. The altar was for constant use, especially in temple service as generally of stone, though it might be of other materials such as earth, brick, metal, or wood etc. The altar was one of the holy components placed in the tabernacle built by Moses. At each altar God gives specific instructions how and what to do with the stones. In this book, you will find three beings at the altar: God, Man and the Devil. It is your choice who you will meet at the altar. I pray it is God.

What is the purpose of a God altar?

Previously, I stated there are two types of altars: God altars and Baal altars. We will first examine the purpose of a God altar. An altar is a special holy place set aside to commune with God. No one is forced to commune at the altar. It is a voluntary place of worship. It is here where one will find salvation and atonement. Salvation means to be saved from sin; to be forgiven and pardoned by God. Therefore, what is sin? Sin in Hebrew means to miss the mark; to disobey or break divine law. It is to reject the law or will of God and substitute it with self (man's) will. This sin (disobedience) will cause separation (break fellowship) between God and mankind, thus requiring the need for salvation and atonement. Atonement in Hebrew means to cover, placate, cancel, explicate, cleanse, forgive, be merciful, pardon, reconcile, and purge.

The Old Testament altar of God

In the Old Testament, God provided altar sacrifices as a way of salvation and atonement for the rich and poor. Whenever an Israelite wanted to approach God, an offering or a sacrifice was brought. In the book of Leviticus chapters 1-7, you will find specific guidelines for sacrifices. These are the different types of appropriate sacrifices and offering.

1. Burnt offerings (Heb. olah) Lev. 1:1-17: This is the most important among all sacrifices. It was to symbolize Israel desire to get rid of its sinful act against God. It had to be an acceptable sacrifice of specific animal descent. It was to be a male animal without spot or blemish; a bull (1:5-9) or a male sheep or goat

21

(1:10-13), or turtledove or young pigeon (1:14-18) which was chosen according to the wealth of the individual. The animal was killed and the blood was drained to pay the penalty of death instead of man for sinning (missing the mark). The blood was very significant, life was taken and blood was shed, without it there could be no remission of sin; it was blood that redeemed the sinner. Confession of sin was made during the sacrifice. This offering was a voluntary expression of complete dedication and consecration to God. It restored and recommitted the broken fellowship between man and God. Only the skin was given to the priest. Everything else was consumed by fire.

2. Grain offering (Heb. minhah) Lev. 2:1-16: This offering signified homage, gratitude and thanksgiving to God. There were four different types under this heading. Fine flour (2:1-3); Unleavened baked cakes (2:4); Unleavened baked pancakes (2:5-6); Unleavened frying pancakes (2:7-9). A portion was consumed by fire the rest was given to the priest.

3. Peace or Fellowship offering (Heb. shelem) Lev. 3:1-17: This offering expressed love and harmony with God for blessing and deliverance. It was a communal meal shared with God, the priest and other worshippers. It was also of animal descent, male or female without blemish; cattle (3:1-6) or lamb (3:7-11) or goat (3:12-17).

4. Sin offering (Heb. hattat) Lev. 4:1-35: This offering was atonement for sins committed through ignorance, especially when restitution is impossible. To sin was to transgress the law and to break any one of the commandments which incurred a penalty. The sacrifice was an animal without blemish merited by the person who sinned. The high priest was to sacrifice a bull (4:3-12), congregation a bull (4:13-21), rulers a male goat (4:22-26), a commoner a female goat or a female lamb (4:27-35), in cases of poverty two turtledoves or two young pigeons (one for a sin offering the other a burnt offering) (5:7-10), in extreme poverty fine flour was used as a substitute (5:11-13). The fatty portion was to be burned as the burnt offering (4:8-10, 19, 26, 31, and 35). The remainder of the bull was to be burned outside the camp when the offering was for the high priest or

congregation (4:11, 12, 20-21). The remainder of the goat or lamb was eaten in the tabernacle court when the offering was for a ruler or commoner (6:26). This offering was compulsory.

5. Trespass offering (Heb. asham) Lev. 5:1-19: There were three conditions where one needed atonement. They were failing to speak the truth; touching any animal or person unclean, speaking profanity or swearing rashly, then, forgetting it was done. The sacrifice was a sheep or goat for the rich, pigeons of turtledoves for the poor, flour for the extremely poor. If the offense was against the Lord or a man, a ram without blemish and restitution according to the priest estimate of the value of the trespass plus one-fifth, (5:15, 16). Remainder of fatty part burned in the altar of burnt offering.[1]

The New Testament altar of God

In the Old Testament to break, one law was sin and incurred a penalty, punishable by death, so a sacrifice was needed to die in place of the human life. In the

---

1 The Nelson Women's Study Bible NKJV; pages 174-175, The Offerings of the Lord.

New Testament, God provided the ultimate sacrifice for all humanity. His son was the sacrificial lamb without spot or blemish. *For God so loved the world, that He gave His only begotten Son, that whosoever believeth in him should not perish, but have everlasting life* (John 3:16). In the New Testament Jesus became the ultimate sacrifice (sin offering) that reconciled humanity back to God. No one else could do it, no one else was found righteous. Jesus is the Lamb of God; He sacrificed his blood and body at Calvary for our sins. Jesus bore our sins (Rom. 6:23), he took the penalty (death) that we deserved (II Cor. 5:21). When he died, the veil was torn in half (Matt. 27:51). This broke the barrier between God and man, which gives us direct access to Him through Jesus Christ. It is a promise of forgiveness and pardon for your sins to all that trust and believes his word (Rom. 5:8, 9). Jesus death on the cross did what sacrificed lambs could not do. His death erased our sin not for a year as done in the Old Testament, but for eternity. The cross did what man could not do. It granted us the privileged to talk with, love and even live with God."

We must understand how important the blood of Jesus is to humanity. When the last plague was pronounced on Egypt, Moses told all of Israel to kill a lamb and cover the lintel of the doorposts with the blood. When the death angel comes to kill all the firstborn of Egypt it would pass over them (Ex. 12:1-13). This is what Jesus blood does for us. His blood protects us from our sins and His blood covers us from death and gives us life. When the Devil also comes to call on us about our past sins, we're protected by the blood of Jesus. When the Devil sees the blood has been applied to our life, he has to pass over us. We are overcomers by the blood of the Lamb and our testimony of it (Rev. 12:11). It is the blood that redeems, forgives, cleanses and justifies us (Rom. 5:6-9).

At the New Testament altar, we are the living sacrifice. The old sinful nature is crucified and buried in Christ. The believer must search his heart and confess any unrepented sin, and wash oneself in the water of the word. The purpose of the altar is to kill off those things dwelling inside of your heart, mind, and flesh that resist the will of God. The things that is contrary to the word of God, which prevents you from serving God to your fullest potential. You are the sacrifice who lay's on the altar so God may perform his perfect work in you. (Romans 12:1-3; Matt. 16:24-26).

Who should build a God altar?

Every nation, every country, every city, every town, every church or worship place, every family, and every person should have a personal altar.

Where a God altar should be built?

An altar should be built everywhere a believer resides and worships. We should visit our personal altars daily.

What can we do at the God altar?

Prayer is a key element at the altar. Prayer is fellowship and communion with God. It is a conversation of the heart with Him. Prayer is having an audience with God and it connects the soul of man with Him. The believer also can read and meditate on the Word of God. Make melody in your hearts. Repent and lay uncover before God, speaking in your heavenly language. Receive guidance, knowledge, purpose and vision for your life (John 4:25). Plan out your work for Christ which is to do the will of the Father (John 4:34).

The Altars Test and Trial of Faith

A t each God altar, you will find a test and trial.

A. Heaven has made a declaration about your earthly stand. This statement is a positive decree about your character and personality. This statement is to declare what truly resides in the inner self (heart and mind).

1. It is tested to show who you are and to whom you belong. The declaration is tried to see if it will remain the same under pressure.

2. The test examines your character and self worth. Is your character a portrait of love, joy, peace, goodness, gentleness and forgiveness?

3. The trial is to determine your trust and obedience to God. It wants to examine your degree of righteousness (right standing) and dependency upon God.

At each altar, heaven has made a declaration about your earthly stand. This declaration states the connection and commitment between God and you. This declaration confirms who you are and to whom you belong. It has said this is my beloved child who honors, serves and obeys me out of love and not duty. This child doesn't love God for the possessions granted, but for the intimate relationship of love with Him, therefore this commitment of love is tested to see if it is true and real. <u>This test examines rather your character is depicting the true, genuine, loving authentic inner self or are you perpetrating a fraud</u>. Does your lifestyle line up accordingly with God's Word, His will for your life and heaven's declaration? The test also is the trying of your true identity and self worth. It completely reveals who you really are.

This test of faith reveals two things: <u>First, it shows your self-worth</u>. In order for the Virgin Mary to be accepted for the position, her self-worth had to be pure, holy, untainted, and submissive. Self-worth will determine how valuable you are to God and humanity: therefore, how valuable was the Virgin Mary to God's plan and destiny? Her birth canal was the instrument used for Jesus to enter the earth realm. Her Godly character had to be obedient, and pertaining to the fruit of the spirit. It was through Eve's disobedience, the world was cursed; and through Mary's obedience, the world was redeemed.

Second, it develops your character and depicts what is truly in the heart, whether love and self-control resides. Can you image the ridicule that Joseph and the Virgin Mary had to face in that era, she was with child, but Joseph hadn't touched her? The law said Joseph had every right to put Mary away, but Matt. 1:19-21 AMP makes a declaration about him: And her [promised] husband Joseph, being a just and upright man and not willing to expose her publicly and to shame and disgrace her, decided to repudiate and dismiss (divorce) her quietly and secretly. But as he was thinking this over, behold, an angel of the Lord appeared to him in a dream, saying, Joseph, descendant of David, do not be afraid to take Mary [as] your wife, for that which is conceived in her is of (from, out of) the Holy Spirit. She will bear a Son, and you shall call His name Jesus [the Greek form of the Hebrew Joshua, which means Savior], for He will save His people from their sins [that is, prevent them from failing and missing the true end and scope of life, which is God]. They didn't fight, they quieted themselves, trusted and obeyed God and followed instructions. So there character showed love, obedience, submission and self control. The test doesn't come to destroy you but prove your love and obedience to God. James tells us to rejoice and endure when we are tested so God may perfect us (James 1:2-7).

After the declaration is proven (tested) then it goes on trial. <u>The trial is the examination of your faith. Therefore, what is faith and why do we need? Faith is having absolute trust in and dependency upon God without questioning or doubting His Word and His faithfulness toward you.</u> The trial examines do you really trust God and believe He will do what He said? It asks will you question or doubt His faithfulness toward you. Are you willing to wait on the promise? Will you persevere and endure hardship until you see the manifestation of the promise? Does your will line up with God's will? At the trial, its examination is to determine quality, performance and usefulness of the individual.

The trial at each of these altars is to check your level of absolute trust in God. It examines your area of perseverance and obedience. Will you continue despite opposition? The true question is; will you obey God in difficult times? The trial teaches God is just and faithful at all times. He has given everyone the same measure of faith. He knows exactly who you are and how much pressure you can bear. "...Obey my voice and I will be your God" (Jer. 7:23). He said, "...I will never leave nor forsake you" (Heb. 13:5). In the trial Joseph and Mary gave up their will, obediently picked up there cross and submitted to God's will; so the Messiah could be saved. Satan's hope is for you to fail the test and trial. Israel refused to obey God, so they wandered for forty years until the old generation died out.

There are steps you have to take to get through the trial. Many of us want to use God as a magical genie, stroke him and therefore, our wish is granted. Ask yourself have I prepared for holiness or hell? To successfully come through the test and trial a manifestation has to become evident in your life. This manifestation is a lifestyle of trust and belief in God. It walks circumspectly according to the Word of God. It is the Word that builds confidence to obey whatever God says; no matter how hard or strange it sounds. The Word makes you prepared and sufficient. You have to hear, believe, see, speak, and act on God's Word. The word says faith cometh by hearing and hearing the Word of God. Therefore, I ask what or who are you hearing? Most people by pass the word "believe"; it denotes the heart is purified of all unrighteousness and filled with love and forgiveness. This places the believer in right standing (righteousness) with God. This righteousness brings about favor of God on your behalf. Now it is not enough to have faith (belief and trust), in God. You have to see in the spiritual realm that it is hope for you to be transformed in this earthly realm. The Word permits you to see it before you see the physical manifestation of it. You have to combine faith with action. In order to be saved you have to believe by hearing the Word, but also you must confess (speak and act on) salvation. Faith without works (right action) is dead. James 2:14-26 NKJV states, "What does it profit, my brethren, if someone says he has faith but does not have works? Can faith save him? If a brother or sister is naked and destitute of daily food, and one of you says to them, "Depart in peace, be warmed and filled," but you do not give them the things which are needed for the body, what does it profit? Thus also faith by itself, if it does not have works, is dead. But someone will say, "You have faith, and I have works." Show me your faith without your works, and I will show you my faith by my works. You believe that there is one God. You do well. Even the demons believe—and tremble! But do you want to know, O foolish man, that faith without works is dead? Was not Abraham our father justified by works when he offered Isaac his son on the altar? Do you see that faith was working together with his works, and by works faith was made perfect? And the Scripture was fulfilled which says, "Abraham believed God, and it was accounted to him for righteousness." And he was called the friend of God. You see a man is justified by works, and not by faith only. Likewise, was not Rahab the harlot also justified by works when she received the messengers and sent them out another way? For as the body without the spirit is dead, so faith without works is dead also." So here I am challenging you after you prayed, heard from God get up and do something. The manifestation won't drop from the sky. It is here in the earthly realm and requires action to be released.

So let's examine what God and heaven declared about some of the bible characters. Each declaration is underlined below. What was the declaration made about Abraham? Gen. 12:2-3 states, "<u>And I will make of thee a great nation, and I will bless thee, and make thy name great; and thou shalt be a blessing: And I will bless them that bless thee, and curse him that curseth thee: and in thee shall all families of the earth be blessed</u>. God promised Abraham and his barren wife Sarah that they would have a son. This son was too be birthed from Sarah's womb. When Abraham began to grow old he and his wife struggled with the fulfillment of the declaration made. He and his wife decided that Abraham would have a son (Ishmael) by Sarah's maidservant (Hagar the Egyptian) to fulfill the promise (Gen. 16). It was an incorrect act and caused much confusion. How could the promised child's heritage be part Egyptian if Jesus was to come from a pure Jewish lineage? God let them know Ishmael wasn't the promise seed and His word would be fulfilled regardless of his age; therefore Abraham failed the test, but later he got it right. He had Isaac, the promised seed (Gen. 21); and his faith went on trial when he was told to sacrifice his son. Abraham didn't doubt but obeyed. How could the promise be fulfilled if he killed the seed? It wasn't his job to worry about the outcome. It was his job to have faith in God and obediently submit to what He said. His obedience was noted and God put the ram in the bush for a sacrificial offering (Gen. 22).

What was the declaration made to Noah? Genesis 6:9 AMP, "…Noah was a just and righteous man, blameless in his [evil] generation; Noah walked [in habitual fellowship] with God." During Noah's time all the people had become extremely evil and rebellious, they sought fulfillment away from God. Therefore God decided to destroy everyone and everything by flooding the earth except Noah and his family. Now Noah's test and trial was would his character remain loving, righteous and blameless when God told him He was going to destroy the earth. The trial was would he stand alone, would he obey and submit to God, would he have self control

36

while being ridiculed, would his faith stand the test, would he continue to be faithful, would he endure?

The final conclusion was Noah's faith stood the test and trial so he and his family's life were spared. The completed task took Noah many, many years to build the ark and it is estimated he remained inside another 377 days. He endured, he persevered, and he prevailed with patience. He led a disciplined lifestyle. When Noah came out the ark he built an altar and worshipped God (Gen. 8:20). This act shows forth his love, honor and devotion. God established a covenant (promise) with Noah that He would never again destroy the earth by a flood. The rainbow is the visible sign given by God (Gen. 9:8-18).

What was Job's declaration? Job 1:1-12 AMP God bragged highly about Job to the Devil: v. 1:7-8 And the Lord said to Satan, "From where did you come?" Then Satan answered the Lord, "From going to and fro on the earth and from walking up and down on it." And the Lord said to Satan, "Have you considered My servant Job, <u>that there is none like him on the earth, a blameless and upright man, one who [reverently] fears God and abstains from and shuns evil [because it is wrong]</u>?"

The devils accusation was Job served God because of all the favor He had granted him. If He would take the hedge from around Job, his family and all his possessions and permit the Devil to cause havoc in his life, he would curse God and die. Well history tells us Job kept his faith in God until his change came. He was faithful through death, turmoil, hardship and even abandonment. His faith withstood the test and trial.

Our last character was Jesus and the declaration made about him was: John 1:29-34 states, "The next day John seeth Jesus coming unto him, and saith. <u>Behold the Lamb of God, which taketh away the sin of the world</u>. This is he of whom I said. After me cometh a man which is preferred before me: for he was before me. And I knew him not: but that he should be made manifest to Israel, there forth am I come baptizing with water. And John bare record saying, I saw the Spirit descending from heaven like a dove, and it abode upon him. And I knew him not: but he that sent me to baptize with water, the same said unto me. <u>Upon whom thou shalt see the Spirit descending, and remaining on him, the same is he which baptizeth with the Holy Ghost. And I saw, and bare record that this is the Son of God.</u>" Also in Matt.

3:17 it attested, "And lo a voice from heaven, saying, This is my beloved Son, in whom I am well pleased."

By now you should recognize that the declaration is made, and it is tested. Many times the Devil will tempt you by making accusations and lies about the word, the promise and the individual's character. Also below you will see Jesus withstand the test and the trial of His faith. He will not compromise his character or the word. He showed absolute trust and obedience toward God. Matt. 4:1 states, "Then was Jesus led up of the Spirit into the wilderness to be tempted of the devil." The first device the Devil used was to bring doubt about whom, He was (his sonship), in addition he wanted Jesus to prove His position and perform a miracle. ...He said, "If thou be the Son of God, command that these stones be made bread." But Jesus answered and said, "It is written Man shall not live by bread alone, but by every word that proceedeth out of the mouth of God (Matt. 4:3-4)." Jesus did not entertain the Devil or his accusations; He stated what the word said. Unlike Esau, He did not let his flesh dictate His blessing or His future.

Then the Devil taketh him up into the holy city, and setteth him on a pinnacle of the temple. And saith unto him, "If thou be the Son of God, cast thyself down: for it is written, He shall give His angels charge concerning thee: and in their hands they shall bear thee up, lest at any time thou dash thy foot against a stone (Matt.4:5-6)." Again he tries to implant doubt and attempt to twist the Word and demands Jesus to demonstrate God's love and protection for Him. Jesus said unto him, "It is written again, "Thou shalt not tempt the Lord thy God (Matt. 4:7)." Again Jesus, full of wisdom, stated the Word and wasn't persuaded by the Devil's foolishness.

Again the Devil taketh him up into an exceeding high mountain, and showeth him all the kingdoms of the world, and the glory of them; And saith unto him, "All these things will I give thee, if thou wilt fall down and worship me (Matt. 4:8-9)." Finally he tries to bribe Jesus with worldly possessions and kingdoms if He will submit and obey. Then saith Jesus unto him, "Get thee hence, Satan: for it is written, Thou shalt worship the Lord thy God, and him only shalt thou serve." Then the devil leaveth him and behold, angels came and ministered unto him (Matt. 4:10-11). Don't be deceived if the devil gives you something there is a high price to pay, which the captivity of your soul is.

I must ask; do you know the declaration heaven is making to you? He loved us so much <u>he declared man was made in His image and likeness</u> (Gen. 1:26). It declares sonship and gives rights and privileges as children. Romans 8:14-18 states, "<u>For as many as are led by the Spirit of God, they are the sons of God. For ye have not received the spirit of bondage again to fear; but ye have received the Spirit of adoption, whereby we cry, Abba, Father. The Spirit itself beareth witness with our spirit, that we are the children of God: And if children, then heirs with Christ; heirs of God, and joint-heirs with Christ; if so be that we suffer with him, that we may be glorified together. For I reckon that the sufferings of this present time are not worthy to be compared with the glory which shall be revealed in us.</u>" One of the rights sonship has given us is righteousness through Jesus Christ. This brings us into relationship and fellowship with the Father. For He hath made him to be sin for us, who knew no sin; that we might be made the righteousness of God in him. Jesus took on our sins so our sonship gives us the privilege to be righteous when we accept Him. So heaven declares we are righteous.

Righteousness permits us to stand in God's presence guilt free. The very thing the enemy doesn't want said about us is we are righteous, something he can never be. If he can contaminate this right standing with inferiority, he can make us feel shame and not worthy to come into God's presence; therefore we break fellowship with Him.

He further said of us in Ephesians 1:3-5, Blessed be the God and Father of our Lord Jesus Christ, who hath blessed us with every spiritual blessing in the heavenly places in Christ: According as he hath chosen us in him before the foundation of the world, that we should be holy and without blame before him in love: Having predestinated us unto the adoption of children by Jesus Christ to himself, according to the good pleasure of his will. Heaven has declared we are special, extraordinary and wonderful in the sight of God. Moreover, we are his children, and if an earthly father will give good gifts to his child how much more will he do as a heavenly father (Luke 11:11-13). In addition the Lord states in John 15:13, "Greater love hath no man than this; that a man lay down his life for his friends. Ye are my friends, if ye do whatsoever I command you." So as you grow closer to God you too will be tested and put on trial. The key is to love and obey God with all your heart, mind and soul in order to pass.

In my conclusion we are not given a time limit when we began the test or the trial so the key is to endure; don't faint; don't give up at the last minute or you will repeat the process again. Don't take this testing or trial personally; it is how we grow spiritually. God is just and fair, He will not test you beyond your means. Abraham, Job and Jesus were all tested and came out as pure gold. Job stated during his trial, "Though he slay me, yet will I trust Him (Job 13:15)." In direct obedience to God, Abraham walked up the mount to sacrifice his son and he became the father of all nations; Job suffered the death of his children and many afflictions yet he endured and was granted more than he had; Jesus went to the cross suffering great humiliation and cruelty, yet He obeyed and sits on the right hand of the Father. This wasn't an easy task for any of them, it was a struggle but the blessing and empowerment came after each one endured. Fight through, persevere through, praise through the struggle. It is the Holy Ghost fire that burns up everything negative in your life and now manifests itself into a blessing which is the result of passing the test and enduring the trial. What was hurtful and harmful now works for your good and becomes ministry that is shared with the world. Abraham became the father of all nations, Job's life of endurance is a testimony to all, and Jesus became the Savior of the world. Each one was tried, yet they trusted in God's faithfulness toward them, so they endure hardship as a good soldier and completed their test and trial. Don't despise the struggle, pain and hardship. It comes to make you; therefore rejoice (praise) for it comes to elevate and promote you. The verdict of the trial comes back as victory. If you stand the test, and stand under the pressure and endure this season of difficult times, promotion and victory are inevitable. James stated, "Blessed is the man that endureth temptation: for when he is tried, he shall receive the crown of life, which the Lord hath promised to them that love him" (James 1:12). I will give more details and examples on faith at the fourth altar.

What is a Baal altar?

The Devil also sets up altars, but his are false altars. Everything God does the Devil will set up a counterfeit system. His goal is to appear to have the same power as the true and living God. False altars are places where idols are worshipped. The fool says in his heart there is no God (Ps. 14:1).

Baal (Hebrew means lord, master, husband) was considered to be the male sun god worshipped and adored in western Asia. This idol was the chief deity among the heathen nations. He was the supreme male divinity of the Phoenician and Canaanites. He is also found among the Moabites and the Midianites (Num. 25:1-3). His altars and sanctuaries were always located on high places, especially high mountains to get the first view of the rising sun, and the last view of the going down of it (Num. 22:41; 23:14; 23:28). The sacrifices made on the Baal altars were animals and humans (Jer. 7:31-34, 19:4-5; II Kings 16:3). These altars were desecrated with obscene and lucrative sexual acts (Ez. 16:15-34. Other Baal gods are Baal-berith, god of covenant (Judges 8:33; 9:4); Baalzebub, god of flies (II Kings 1:2-6, 16).[2]

Israel was always letting other foreign nations affect their relationship with God. They sold out to the flesh instead of holding onto the promise. During Moses, absence and delay Israel persuaded Aaron to participate in making an idol to worship. They decided to denounce God and make a golden calf of gold. They said, *"These be thy god, O Israel, which brought thee up out of the land of Egypt."* This idol was a representation of the Egyptian god, a young bull called Apis, worshipped near the land of Goshen. All gods had their consecrated women who performed immoral acts. These are the sins of Aaron and Israel after building the idol: built an altar, made a proclamation to worship, called a feast, offered burnt and peace offerings, permitted eating and drinking of the sacrifice, singing, dancing and honoring

---

[2] The Dake Annotated Reference Bible KJV, p. 452 letter x; and p. 182 The Bible Facts About False Gods #5 (2-5).

the god. Israel along with the priests fell into a totally backslidden condition heavily leading towards apostasy. God would have destroyed the nation if Moses had not interceded on their behalf. Their outright disregard and disrespect for God and sin was exposed and penalized (Ex. 32:1-35). Israel participated in these practices while in Egypt (Josh. 24:14; Ez. 20:8; 23:3-8). When testing times came, they reverted to these heathen practices.[3]

When Joshua led Israel into the promise land, each tribe was given specific instructions. They were to drive out all the inhabitants of the land. Not all the tribes obeyed these directions. Some tribes permitted the Canaanites to stay, so they made treaties with their enemies. They were told not to intermingle with them or worship there gods. Israel rejected God, joined the Canaanites, became a harlot, and filled their altars with false gods. God instructed Israel to tear down the pagan altars. After a visitation from an angel, they repented and served God until Joshua died. After Joshua's death, the next unlearned generations returned to idolatry (Judges 2).

---

[3] The Dake Annotated Reference Bible, p. 156, d and e

And the children of Israel <u>did evil</u> in the sight of the Lord, and served Baalim (plural of Baal): And <u>they forsook the Lord</u> God of their fathers, which brought them out of the land of Egypt, and <u>followed other gods</u>, of the gods of the people that were round about them, and bowed themselves unto them, and <u>provoked the Lord to anger</u>. And they <u>forsook the Lord, and served Baal and Ashtoreth</u> (Judges 2:11-13).

So God decides to rise up judges to help Israel, but they still didn't listen to sound counsel; thus, they turned quickly away from God, and went back into idolatry. God allowed other nations to remain in the land; this became a problem for Israel (Judges 2:14-23).

This practice of Baal continued to spread heavily during the reign of the kings. Temples were erected and priests appointed. It was a blatant disregard for God's commandment given to Israel. Jezebel, daughter of Ethbaal (meant with Baal), king of Sidon furthered the caused when she married Ahab, Israel's eighth king. Ahab permitted Jezebel to introduce Baal worship in their homes, the temples and finally to the nation. During this marriage, Jezebel influenced Ahab to adopt and formalize her religion. She transplanted her idolatry into the kings and peoples' heart until they bowed and worshipped Baal instead of God (I Kings16:29-33). His wife was so evil she tried to exterminate the entire God ordained prophets and priests (I Kings 18:4) to establish Baal prophets in the palace and temples. Four hundred and fifty prophets of Baal, along with a high number of Asherah (the female moon god) prophets served her (I Kings18:18-19). Of course, burning of incense and offering burnt offerings (Jer. 7:9), sexual perversion (Lev. 20:1-7; I Sam. 2:22), human sacrifices (Jer. 7:31), and the cutting of flesh (I King 18:26-28) was involved in these types of worship ceremonies. This idolatry causes an increasing hardening of the heart and stubbornness of mind as it continues.

The battle at the altar between God's Prophet and Baal's Prophet Jezebel purposely demanded that her god Baal be considered equal with God. It was the prophet Elijah, on Mount Caramel who showed that Baal was no match for the true and living God. These are the words recorded in I King 18:20-40 WSB, NKJV), *So Ahab sent for all the children of Israel, and gathered the*

prophets together on Mount Carmel. And Elijah came
to all the people, and said, "*How long will you falter
between two opinions? If the Lord is God follow Him;
but if Baal, follow him.*" But the people answered him
not a word. Then Elijah said to the people, I alone am
left a prophet of the Lord; but Baals prophets are four
hundred and fifty men. Therefore let them give us two
bulls; and let them choose one bull for themselves, cut
it in pieces, and lay it on the wood, but put no fire under
it; and I will prepare the other bull, and lay it on the
wood, but put no fire under it. *Then you call on the name
of your gods, and I will call on the name of the Lord;
and the God who answers by fire, He is God.* So all the
people answered and said, "It is well spoken." Now
Elijah said to the prophets of Baal, "Choose one bull
for yourselves and prepare it first, for you are many;
and call on the name of your god, but put no fire under
it." So they took the bull which was given them, and
they prepared it, and called on the name of Baal from
morning even till noon, saying, "O Baal, hear us!" But
there was no voice; no one answered. Then they leaped
about the altar which they had made.

And so it was, at noon, that Elijah mocked them and said, "Cry aloud, for he is a god; either he is medicating, or he is busy, or he is on a journey, or perhaps he is sleeping and must be awakened." So they cried aloud, and cut themselves, as was their custom, with knives and lances, until the blood gushed out on them. And when midday was past, they prophesied until the time of the offering of the evening sacrifice. But there was no voice; no one answered, no one paid attention.

Then Elijah said to all the people, "Come near to me." So all the people came near to him. And he repaired the altar of the Lord that was broken down. And Elijah took twelve stones, according to the number of the tribes of the sons of Jacob, to whom the word of the Lord had come, saying, "Israel shall be your name." Then with the stones he built an altar in the name of the Lord; and he made a trench around the altar large enough to hold two seahs of seed. And he put the wood in order, cut the bull in pieces, and laid it on the wood, and said, "Fill four water pots with water, and pour it on the burnt sacrifice and on the wood." Then he said, "Do it a second time," and they did it a second time; and he said, "Do it a third time," and they did it a third time. So the water ran all around the altar; and he also filled the trench with water. And it came to pass, at the time of the offering of the evening sacrifice, that Elijah the prophet came near and said, "Lord God of Abraham, Isaac, and Israel, let it be known this day that You are God in Israel and I am Your servant, and that I have done all these things at Your word. Hear me, O Lord, hear me, that this people may know that You are the Lord God, and that You have turned their hearts back to You again."

Then the fire of the Lord fell and consumed the burnt sacrifice, and the wood and stones and the dust, and it licked up the water that was in the trench. Now when all the people saw it, they fell on their faces; and they said. "The Lord, He is God! The Lord, He is God!"

And Elijah said of them, "Seize the prophets of Baal! Do not let one of them escaped!" So they seized them; and Elijah brought them down to the Brook Kishon and executed them there.

Another person I would like to discuss under these Baal altars is Balaam (Num. 22-25). He was a "seer of the gods" (a soothsayer, fortuneteller, witch doctor) the son of Beor (Joshua 13:22). King Balak, a Baal worshipper who presided over Moab became fearful of the Israelites, so he summoned Balaam's help. The king feared the Israelites would takeover his territory, therefore, he offered Balaam money to curse God's people (Israel). Balaam proceeded with this mission but was interrupted by an angel of the Lord. The angel ordered Balaam to bless Israel instead of cursing them. Although he wanted to defy the almighty and all-powerful God, he could not. He blessed the people on three occasions (Num 24:10). When that didn't work, he told Balak if the women could seduce the Israelites into immorality and idolatry (Num. 25:1-3), God would curse them (Numbers 25:1-9 read story). He was finally killed by the Israelites (Num. 31:8).

1ST ALTAR FAITH IN GOD

PURPOSE: SEEK TO KNOW HIM!

BETHEL - HOUSE OF GOD
GEN. 28:19-23

Personal relationship established with God

Jacob laid on the rock (Jesus Christ). Here he laid down his burdens. "...*Upon this rock, I will build my church and the gates of hell shall not prevail*" (Mt. 16:18). He also learned God was with him. Up until now, Isaac assumed religious responsibility for his entire family. He was growing old and it is now time for his son to become responsible and develop his own personal relationship with God.

Altar of

Sacrifice-redeems and restores

Submission-establishes a covenant with God

Salvation-establishes a relationship with Jesus

This altar defines:

1. Who You Are!

2. Whose You Are!

Loves and Honors God and Self

Personal: Salvation and the Atoning Blood of Jesus Christ. The outer man is saved which is an outward sign of repentance. At this altar, a sacrifice is made to open the door for salvation. This altar deals with the outer man; this is a representation of the outer court in the tabernacle. Here in the Old Testament, the priest had to offer a burnt offering, which was a lamb without spot, or blemish to atone for sin. Without the shedding of blood there could be no remission of sin.

In the New Testament Jesus Christ is the sacrificial lamb who died to redeem and restore humanity back to His Father (God). The corruption of the flesh is in the blood. When we accept Christ, we are covered or infused with His blood. It is the blood that washes, cleanses and makes us whole; it is nothing but the blood of Jesus. The old man dies and the new man is born again or regenerated.

Salvation and the new birth: In Jacob's quest to find himself at the altar, he had to deal with his identity, carnal mind and nature. Jacob is the righteousness of God. So there were things in him that had to die and be buried [all his unrighteousness (trickery and deception)]. It is here we lay down our old sinful, rebellious and independent nature. Also there were things that needed to be resurrected [his responsibility and obligation to love and serve God]. Jacob had a legal right to establish a personal relationship with God and to walk according to the established covenant. This altar is a personal relationship altar. No one can come for you. The goal is to bring deliverance from family, traditions and generational curses.

Test: to remove those things that are not pleasing to God, and receive those things God deems necessary for you to fulfill His will.

Trial: so He may be able to get total glory out of your life.

CHANGE YOUR NAME!
Change Me

Jacob's name meant supplanter, cheater or deceiver. After his conversion, his name was changed to Israel. When you receive Christ in your life, your name will be changed also. Your name was good enough for where you were but not good for where you are going. Your new name releases you from your past and the Devil can no longer hold you hostage in this area. Therefore if any man be in Christ, he is a new creature (new creation): old things are passed away; behold, all things are become new (II Cor. 5:17). Isaiah further talked about newness in 43:18-19 NKJV he stated, "Do not remember the former things, nor consider the things of old. Behold I will do a new thing, now it shall spring forth; shall you not know it? I will make a road in the wilderness, and rivers in the desert." This new name transcends you into a new realm of blessings, dominion and authority. It is here our sinful rebellious, independent nature is killed and a nature of salvation, submission and dependency emerges. If you are reading this book, God is calling you into repentance right now.

You are Saved and Delivered from People.

We clearly see in this text that the bible speaks to the carnal as well to the spiritual man. It portrays the light and dark side of our character. By divine intervention, the generational curse was broken once again. Everything born comes from a seed. Abraham, Isaac and Jacob wives were all barren. Many think that mishaps and unfavorable conditions are God's way of punishing them, but in actuality, it is the devil trying to abort destiny, by stealing and killing the seed. He knows if he can steal or kill the seed all the lives following may never reach their destiny in God. Therefore, he afflicts the womb; thus, creating the curse of barrenness (inability to conceive) spiritually and naturally. Often times this kind of curse will affect whole families. We see this in the family history of Abraham, Isaac and Jacob whose wives were barren. The Devil kept coming after the promised Word given to Abraham that his seed would be blessed (Gen 12:1-3).

If we look closely at the bible, the devil has continuously created chaos with the seed: he ordered all firstborn killed during Moses and Jesus' birth; God permitted Moses to be spared and raised in Pharaoh's house. Joseph and Mary had to flee their home to insure the birth of Jesus. Sarah, Rachael and Rebekah were all barren, but through divine intervention, God touched their wombs and Sarah conceived Isaac, Rachael conceived Esau and Jacob, and Rebekah conceived Joseph and Benjamin. In addition, Hannah and Elizabeth were both barren; what if the lives of Samuel, the priest, and John, the beloved disciple was eluded? Or done away? Each of these children was a key character in the bible, which shaped divine purpose and destiny. They were birthed through much prayer.

Isaac was 40 years old when he married. He was sixty when his sons were born. Through prayer, God heard the cry of this woman and blessed the womb of His maidservant. Once Rebekah became pregnant, she inquired (sought) of the Lord because of the struggle that was going on in her womb. The Lord told her the struggle is because there were two nations (twins) inside of her. One shall be stronger than the other, and the older shall serve the younger (Gen. 25:19-27).

We begin the text with a father giving definite instructions to his son. The key to this altar is to LEAVE AND CLEAVE. Salvation is a move: Leave your old nature and ways (plans), cleave to God's purposes, plans, calling, and divine will for your life. Many times, we must leave our families to free ourselves from traditions, strongholds and generational curses to walk in the generational blessing. Abraham in Gen. 12:1-3, and his grandson, Jacob in Gen. 28:1-3, were both told to leave there parents home (change their location), so God could change them internally. Many of us are stuck because we fear the unknown and we refuse to move and take responsibility for ourselves. This responsibility calls us to seek God for ourselves. There are three blessings given to man:

1. Universal-Abrahamic blessing
2. Personal-spiritual gifts and family inherited blessing.

3. Corporate-which is based upon affiliation of church, nationality, and region in which you reside.

Let us journey with Jacob through the scriptures, Gen. 28:3-19 NKJV as he begins this adventure.

V. 1 Jacob was blessed by his father first. This blessing is very important. It calls forth the blessing of God over his life, his future generations' lives and confirms his identity. His blessing stated: *May God Almighty bless you, and make thee fruitful and multiply you, that thou may be an assembly of peoples; And give you the blessing of Abraham, to you and your descendants with you, "That you may inherit the land in which you are a stranger, which God gave to Abraham"* (Gen. 28:3-4 NKJV).

Today's society should be very careful in the choices they make concerning their seed. Today too many of our homes are being run by single parent mothers; thus creating problems with our children's self-identity. A father does not cover them. They are starved for the father's love and blessing upon their lives. Our daughters yearn for a father's touch, and our sons long for an in house mirror (an image, a pattern, blueprint of manhood). Our children are not growing up to be healthy responsible adults, because no father has blessed and declared their true heritage. Jacob's father spoke life and identity in him. If one out every three black males is incarcerated, how will the children learn their identity? Who will speak into their lives? The Devil goes to and fro seeking who is not protected, so he may devour them. Who will protect the children from the wolves of this world? We need our black men free and accountable.

V. 2 He is told, *Arise go* (get up, stop crying, and separate). God is telling us to come to unfamiliar territory and meet Him. Will You Obey God! After the blessing, Jacob was charged; he could not take a wife from his country because the woman worshipped foreign gods and had intermingled with other races. This intermingling became a huge problem for King Solomon because he allowed his foreign wives to worship their foreign gods and idols. He had seven hundred wives and three hundred concubines who in his later days turned his heart away from God (I Kings 11:1-8). The text clearly teaches, *be ye not unequally yoked together with unbelievers: for what fellowship hath righteousness with unrighteousness? and what communion hath light with darkness? And what concord hath Christ with Belial? or what part hath he that believeth with an infidel? And what (agreement) hath the temple of God with idols? for ye are the temple of the living God; as God hath said, I will dwell in them, and walk in them; and I will be their God, and they shall be my people. Wherefore come out from among them, and be ye separate, saith the Lord, and touch not the unclean thing; and I will receive you (II Cor. 6:14-17).* Whatever you join your members to, you can become. To this day this charge holds true God still charges us not to marry unbelievers. *Will you join your members to a harlot? God forbid (I Cor. 6:15-17) You cannot serve two masters (Luke 16:13).*

V. 3-4 This blessing added purpose to him and his descendants (family). It dictates his inheritance, which is connected to his grandfather Abraham's blessing. This blessing is found in Gen. 12:2-3 it states the following: *And I will make of thee a great nation, and I will bless thee, and make thy name great; and thou shall be a blessing: And I will bless them that bless thee, and curse him that curseth thee: and in thee shall all fami-lies of the earth will be blessed*. [Gal. 3:8].

An injustice is done when a child does not know his heritage. He does not know the true lineage purpose and blessing bestow upon the family. Further blessing given to Israel is explained clearly in Duet. 28:1-14. all these blessings are an inheritance to the believer who walks after God and not after the flesh.

V. 5 Rebekah advises her son Jacob to flee to Haran because his brother Esau threatened to kill him (Gen. 27:41-46). She pretended his leaving was to find a wife different from the daughters of Heth. In Gen. 27:1-40 Jacob tricked his father and cheated his older brother Esau out his birthright (a double portion of his father's inheritance) and their father's deathbed blessing (May all your mother's sons bow down to you Gen. 27:29 NASB). He ran from Esau into another life of turmoil and deception. His Uncle Laban, who had him work for fourteen years to marry his daughter Rachel, tricked Jacob the trickster. This lesson is the unchanging law of sowing and reaping. Many times, we blame things on the devil but actually, it is the law of compensation at work returning with dividends what you gave (Gal. 6:7).

V. 10 Jacob left by force. The lesson here questions his obedience. It ask, are you willing to obey God or will circumstances force you to come out from among your circle of familiarity and tradition. Choose you this day whom you shall serve. God has given us a choice to accept or reject Him. He said, whosoever will, let him come. Today is the day of salvation; harden not your heart as they did in the day of provocation (Heb. 3:8). Although it took a crisis for Jacob to leave, he had to go in order to be where he would become totally dependent on God. All alone and alienated from his people was a perfect place where God could speak to him.

V.11 Jacob headed toward Haran and the night repre-sented the dark side of his personality. God now wants him to come to terms with his unrighteousness. Jacob had to learn God for himself. In order to come into the light you must relieve yourself of the turmoil and sin in your life. The light was turned on in Jacob's life. He no longer would stumble over the same thing again.

Therefore, he laid his head down on the rock that is a metaphor for Jesus, Christ. The Lord is calling him to rest (a peaceful and quiet place) so he can hear Him. He said, take my yoke, for it is light and burden free (Matt. 11:28-30). It is time to be grounded into a relationship with Jesus by way of His Word (the Bible). It will give you instructions of furthering this relationship of righteousness through correction and reproof (II Tim. 3:16-17).

V. 12 Here the Lord is telling Jacob, there is an open heaven set before him. The angels are awaiting orders from God to answer his problems. *Whatsoever we bind on earth shall be bound in heaven, and whatsoever we loose on earth shall be loosed in heaven (Matt. 18:18).* Many Christians will continue to see the problem instead of seeing the God who solves all problems. As you can see, there are many adjustments to be made in us at this altar.

V. 13-15 I have made a covenant with you. At this altar, God made a solemn agreement that is binding with Jacob. He recognized the promises God made with his ancestors. Now God is making a continued blessing with him. It stated God would:

1. give the land to him and his seed.

2. multiply, spread and make his seed great.

3. thy seed and all families will be blessed.

4. be with you wherever you go.

5. will bring you back to this land again.

6. will not leave you until I have fulfilled my promises.

God promised Jacob, I will do you good for I love you and your ancestors. This great covenant calls forth blessing, purpose and destiny of his seed. Therefore, it is no surprise why the Devil's attack was always against the seed. His desire is to break the covenant and blessing between man and God. So what personal covenant has God made with you and your family? What is the promise word made for the add last name Family?

V. 16 After Jacob communed with God he woke up and realized God was here in this place with him. Call on God and I guarantee he will answer. He will come in and sup with you. Although your sin be as scarlet he will reason with you, and make them white as snow (Isa. 1:18).

V. 17-19 He feared God and called this place the House of God (Bethel); and this is the gates of heaven. Jacob had a personal encounter with God, and he is in right standing with God. Now his spirit fully understood verse 12 now. He recognized the angels ascending and descending was God's way of setting an open heaven before Him. In addition, God was awaiting his command from the earth realm to reach the heaven realm so he could command the angels to deliver Jacob. We as born again believers have the same power. God stated in His word; Command Ye Me (Isa. 45:11). He is waiting for you to decree and declare what you want, so he can perform it. He set the stones as an altar and a memorial to God. This was Jacob's way of honoring God for His manifested Glory. He set up an altar here at Bethel and consecrated it unto God. Previously, it was a pillow where he laid down his head and burdens, which have now become an altar of communion for a new man and God. The Prophet Elijah also visited this altar.

V. 20-21 Jacob vowed that if God would keep him and return him back home in peace, he would make the Lord his God and give him a tenth of all he received. Jacob served Laban for twenty years and God blessed and kept him. At the appointed time God told Jacob to go back home (Gen. 31). Jacob journeyed home wealthy, but fearful of his brother. Jacob had another encounter with God he wrestled with the angel all night long and refused to let him go until he was blessed. No man was to see God face to face and live (Gen. 32:30).

It is here everyone must deal with the question, Who Am I? This question deals with your self-worth. It states how valuable you are to God and others. It gets to the core of why you exist. It also seals the deal of Whose Am I? I believe this is part of the struggle coming to terms with your self esteem. Will you believe what God has said about you? For He has said, you are a child of God full of love, beauty, glory, splendor and power. Once we believe this about ourselves we begin to see and walk in our true selves. Jacob had outer wealth but now he had to come to terms with his inner wealth and personal relationship with God and himself.

For Jacob the struggle is over and finally he is broken and ready to surrender all unto the Lord. This encounter made Jacob a changed man who now has a changed character. Finally, Jacob's name is changed to Israel, which means God preserves; and his heart was turned totally towards Him. In (Gen. 33:10 NKJV) God upheld his word, and the brothers peacefully reconciled; he fixed everything he had done wrong in his life. Jacob stated, "…I have seen your face as though I had seen the face of God, and you were pleased with me." God fulfilled his promise because out Jacob's loin came the twelve tribes.

It is Christ, who was born, bled and died to give us a brand new start. What a precious gift given to us by none other than a wonderful and gracious Lord and Savior, Jesus Christ. It is at this altar I challenge you to seek the living and holy God. He is the only one who can change you. His desire is to make a covenant with you.

Conclusion: Relationship of Fellowship, change of mind.

1. Make covenant with you.

    a. Becoming one with God.

2. Daily devotion with God.

    a. Open door

    b. Open heaven

The thief cometh not, but to steal, and to kill,
and to destroy (Jn. 1:10).

1ST BAAL ALTAR
SUBTLE MIND CONTROL

PURPOSE: FORCIBLE TAKE OVER
OF THE MIND

When the Devil was put out of heaven, he lost his relationship with God and his authority. Since then the devil is after man's loving relationship with God and others. He is after the head of everything because he lost his position by the head of heaven (God). He made Jesus the head of the church, the man the head of the woman; and the devil is always attacking their leadership. His jealousy seeks to destroy man's authority by way of mind seduction and control. He is constantly attacking the head, of every nation, country, state, city, town, church and family. Your head houses your mind.

Altar of

Disobedience establishes separation to God's Word.

Defiance establishes a spirit of

stubbornness and resistance.

Death establishes a relationship with the Devil.

This altar seeks

1. Control of the Mind.

God's way of dealing with us is through the mind and heart. We must guard the entrance of our mind and heart. For to be carnally minded is death; but to be spiritually minded is life and peace. Because the carnal mind is enmity against God: for it is not subject to the law of God, neither indeed can be (Romans 8:6-7). In the Gk. Sarx; carnal denotes flesh, the entire nature of man, sense and nature are without the Holy Spirit. Proverbs states, "Watch over your heart with all diligence, for from it flows the springs of life" (4: 23 NASB).

The mind is the seat of thought and memory: the center of consciousness that generates thoughts, feelings, ideas and perceptions; it stores knowledge and memories; the capacity to think, understand and reason. The Devil chooses to control the mind. It is the central control center (computer or switchboard). It is where all information is processed and stored through the power of thoughts. Thinking controls all behavior, control the mind and you control it. <u>The Devil cannot takeover your mind without your permission.</u> It is the doorway to your inner man: heart, mind and soul.

The first attack of Satan is in the mind. Once the Devil enters your mind, he implants a disease (virus) into the memory of the computer (mind) which is intended to interrupt God's true vision and purpose for your life. This virus disrupts and disconnects the memory board. It transmits information that separates you from God and His love. The motive is to cause non-dependency upon Him. This new program permits you to act independently from your creator and truth. The true purpose of this disease is to set up strongholds or fortresses in your mind. When you dwell on things that are not of God, contrary to His word and way, or fantasize evil, you give the enemy a place to erect a stronghold or fortress. A stronghold is a stubborn idea or opinion that opposes the will of God. Moreover, the bible states you can resist these strongholds, "For though we walk (live) in the flesh, we are not carrying on our warfare according to the flesh and using mere human weapons. For the weapons of our warfare are not physical [weapons of flesh and blood], but they are mighty before God for the overthrow and destruction of strongholds, [Inasmuch as we] refute arguments and theories and reasonings and every proud and lofty thing that sets itself up against the [true] knowledge of God; and we lead every thought and purpose away captive into the obedience of Christ (the Messiah, the Anointed One) (II Corinthians 10:3-5 AMP).

Satan's strategy is to besiege your mind, erode your resistance and capture your thoughts. The Devil wants you to become confused and passive so he can do a forcible takeover in this weak condition. Never let anyone tinker with your mind. Do not let anyone tell you to let your mind drift. The Devil desires you to give up your power of thought, he is subtle and crafty. He never announces who he is unless you desire to talk with him first. He will drop suggestions into your mind. He will use the power of persuasion or trickery to get you to agree with his deceptive process. The Devil used deception by twisting the Word of God until Adam and Eve gave up their power of truth and agreed with him. The Devil played with Eve's mind and it cost her dearly. He caused Adam to know disobedience, defiance and death. The Devil came after the implanted Word of the mind. He came after three impartations given to man by God:

      1. His relationship,

      2. His position,

      3. His Word.

...And God said, "Let Us make man in Our image, according to Our likeness; let them have dominion...Be fruitful and multiply; fill the earth and subdue it: and have dominion... (Genesis 1:24-28 NKJV).

1. A relationship is a significant connection or similarity between two or more things, to connect, to unite (Gen. 1:27-28, 2:7, 18-25). God with mankind is the highest form relationship that has ever existed. He calls us into right relationship (connection) and fellowship (communion) with Him. It was God who created, formed

and shaped man (1:26-27, 2:7). Relationship can manifest itself to be good or bad, healthy or unhealthy. The second relationship established by Him was marriage (the covenant union between male and female 2:22-24). Out this relationship came all others. The third relationship was between parent and child (4:1). Man was not meant to live alone (2:18). We are designed to love one another through relationship (everybody needs somebody). Man's true love can transform and bring relationship under subjection and submission. There was no relationship established with things, he was told to have dominion and subdue them (not people). It's time to put first things first, relationships instead of material things.

The Devil cannot harm God, so he fights what is closely related to Him, which is mankind. He knows man is the apple of God's eye (made in his image and likeness) and he was created to commune with Him. He ruined his relationship with God so his desire is to destroy everything connected to God. His goal is to nullify man's significant loving connection between: God and mankind, a husband and wife; a parent and a child; siblings; friendships etc. He wants every relationship to be filled with disobedience and defiance, so he will pit one person against another. The Devil knows everything multiplies by way of a seed (Gen. 1:22-28), so his goal is to kill mankind's chance of reproduction and relations. He wants to destroy the man's seed and create barrenness in the women's womb. Therefore, he will use all forms of trickery to create a chaotic environment for mankind. He also knew man was given headship over all relationships; and if the man is out of order, everything birthed from him will be out of order. We are a product of God; therefore our lives were designed to create. The parent has the power to form and shape the child through proper leadership and conditioning.

2. The Devil rebelled and was kicked out heaven; he lost his position and authority (Rev. 12:7-9). Therefore, he will do everything to create the same for man. He created circumstances for the man to be kicked out the garden and lose his position of right standing and his authority granted to him by God (Gen. 3). His ultimate goal is to have everyone miss heaven, become doomed to hell and become a part of his kingdom (Hab. 2:5; Isa. 5:13-14). He thought he did that when he caused separation between God and Adam, but it didn't worked.

Later in the text God restored and reconciled mankind back to Him.

3. The Devil is always after the Word promised to mankind by God. When God speaks, there always will be a manifestation. "...Man shall not live by bread alone, but by every word that proceedeth out of the mouth of God" (Matt. 4:4). He knows the word is a lamp unto our feet and it lights our way (Ps. 119:105). He will do anything to keep man in darkness. He wants you to be ignorant of the Word and his devices. Despite the Devil's plan, God has granted the believer so many promises in the Word of God. The bible is our handbook to a successful and victorious life. He told us, "to meditate in the word day and night" (Ps. 1:2). He also said to, "ask and it shall be given; seek and we shall find; knock and doors will be opened" (Mt. 7:7).

In the history of creation, Genesis chapter one NKJV, God recorded on:

Day 1-*Then God said, "Let there be light"; and there was light. And God saw the light, that it was good... (v. 3-4).*

Day 2-*And God called the dry land Earth, and the gathering together of the waters He called Seas. And God saw that <u>it was good</u> (v. 10).*

Day 3-*And the earth brought forth grass, the herb that yields seed according to its kind, and the tree that yields fruit whose seed is in itself according to its kind. And God saw that <u>it was good</u> (v. 12).*

Day 4-*Then God made two great lights: the greater light to rule the day, and the lesser light to rule the night. He made the stars also. God set them in the firmament of the heavens to give light on the earth, and to rule over the day and over the night, and to divide the light from the darkness. And God saw that <u>it was good</u> (v. 16, 17).*

Day 5-*So God created great sea creatures, and every living thing that moves, with which the waters abounded, according to their kind, and every winged bird according to its kind. And God saw that <u>it was good</u> (v. 21).*

Day 6-*And God made the beast of the earth according to its kind, cattle according to its kind, and everything that creeps on the earth according to its kind. And God saw that <u>it was good</u>. Then God said, Let Us make man in Our image, according to Our likeness; let them have dominion over the fish of the sea, over the birds of the air, and over the cattle, over all the earth and over every creeping thing that creeps on the earth." So God created man in His own image; in the image of God He created him; male and female He created them. Then God blessed them, and God said to them, "Be fruitful and multiply; fill the earth and subdue it; have dominion over the fish of the sea, over the birds of the air, and over every living thing that moves on the earth." And God said, "See, I have given you every herb that yields seed which is on the face of all the earth, and every tree whose fruit yields seed; to you it shall be for food. Also, to every beast of the earth, to every bird of the air, and to everything that creeps on the earth, in which there is life, I have given every green herb for food"; and it was so. Then God saw everything that He had made, and indeed <u>it was very good</u>. So the evening and the morning were the sixth day. (V. 25-31).*

Now up to this point all man knew was <u>good</u>, and his thought process was only aware of God-consciousness. There is no higher being or law than God. The Creator made man, in His image and likeness thus making his image and true reflection loving, beautiful but most of all <u>good</u> (James 1:16-17). He wanted to converse with man in his pure and highest form. Man is the righteousness of God, which simply means he is in right standing with God. Righteousness Gk. Tsedeq right, clear self, just. It means morally upright; always behaving according to a religious or moral code; considered to be good, outstanding; justifiable; The Devil did not attack the man right out because he knew Adam loved and valued his relationship with God. His reflection was pure and holy. His spirit knew only God and His righteousness. Up to this point, nothing or no one had penetrated his spirit. His creator has been nothing but loving and kind to him. He has provided Adam a healthy relationship with Himself and the woman, so he would not be along. When examining the above verses everything created and provided for the man was good including the animals and food, therefore it was no reason to distrust or question His Supreme Being or His Word. Adam knew

God therefore; he knew himself and God's word. The Devil could not distort Adam's image of himself because he dwelled in the presence of the true and living God, and He mirrored God's image in a mini form, it had to be mind blowing.

Therefore, the Devil subtly attacks the man through the deception of the woman. In Gen. 2:8, 9 you will find these words recorded; *And the Lord God planted a garden eastward in Eden; and there he put the man whom he had formed. And out of the ground made the Lord God to grow every tree that is pleasant to the sight, and good for food; the tree of life also in the midst of the garden, and the tree of knowledge of good and evil.* This scripture tells us the food on the trees were appealing to the eye and good for food. It also tells us there were two distinct trees in the midst of the garden, with appealing food. First, he told of the tree of life (which if eaten man would live forever 3:22) and secondly, of the tree of knowledge, of good and evil, (which would give man to know good and evil as a result of sin 3:22).

Now according to the King James Version of the bible these are the exact words God said: in Genesis 2:15-17: *And the Lord God took the man and put him into the Garden of Eden to dress it and keep it.* Up until now, everything was under the authority of man, for he governed, as God did. *v. 16 And the Lord God commanded the man, saying, Of every tree of the garden thou mayest freely eat: v. 17 But of the tree of the knowledge of good and evil, thou shalt not eat of it: for in the day that thou eatest thereof thou shalt surely die.* These were God's exact words: Below we will attempt to show where the distortion was. The enemy deceived Eve to believe what her husband and God said was not true and accurate. He played with her mind and the word. He made her feel like God was withholding something good from them. In Gen. 3:1-6 states:

Serpent, v. 3:1: *Now the serpent was more subtle than any beast of the field which the Lord God had made. And he said unto the woman, Yea, hath God said, "Ye shall eat of every tree of the garden?"* First, why was she talking and entertaining the serpent instead of God's Command. She had Adam with whom to talk; wasn't that enough? The first tactic of the Devil is for you to start a dialogue with him. Next he opens the door of doubt by <u>changing and questioning what the word said</u>

(Yea, hath God said, "Ye shall eat of every tree of the garden?)" We are no match for the Devil; so do not talk to him. Speak the Word only and let him take the rest up with Jesus.

The Woman said, v. 3:2, 3: *And the woman said unto the serpent, We may eat of the fruit of the trees of the garden: But of the fruit of the tree which is in the midst of the garden, God hath said, Ye shall not eat of it, <u>neither shall ye touch it</u>, lest ye die.* Now the woman was not accurate when repeating what God said. Look at the scripture above Gen. 2:16-17, God did not say Adam would die if he did not touch it, nor did He say she would die if she touched or ate the fruit. <u>He told Adam he would die if he ate the fruit</u>.

The Serpent said, v. 3:4, 5: *And the serpent said unto the woman, "Ye shall not surely die: For God doth know that in the day ye eat thereof, then your eyes shall be opened, and ye shall be gods, knowing good and evil."* At this point, it became a contradiction of God's command and word. The serpent began to reason with her emotions and desires; thus, nullifying the truth.

The Woman acted, v. 3:6: *And when the woman, saw that the tree was good for food, and that is was pleasant to the eyes, and a tree to be desired to make one wise, she took of the fruit thereof, and did eat,.* She began to compare the fruit to what she had eaten already. She starts coveting the fruit with her eyes. When we covet, we desire the forbidden. The Devil made her feel God had something that would enhance their mind and He was not giving it to them. Now the question is how did she know this fruit would make her like gods and wise? It is obvious that the serpent convinced her that being, as gods would make her wise with independent thoughts and choices. He also persuaded her that God was withholding something good from them, which was to know good and evil. God did not intend for man to know <u>evil</u> (disobedience) or sin (miss the mark). She entertained and played with the serpent until she was seduced by his lusty presentation to eat the fruit. Satan implies doubt, disbelief and finally disobedience to God and His word. With this deceptive tactic, he convinced Eve to eat of the fruit. She ate and Adam said or did nothing. Eve did not understand man was made in God's image and likeness and His Father had a master plan for man's life.

The woman is under the man's authority, and the man is under God's authority. Eve's problem was she became unsubmissive to God, His Word and Adam.

The Man acted, v. 3:6: *and gave also unto her husband with her; and he did eat.* Adam was with Eve the whole time she gave audience to the serpent. Why did Adam leave Eve and himself unguarded? Why did he let her continue the conversation with serpent? Why did he eat the fruit after knowing specifically what the word said? The man was in charge, not the woman, yet Adam permitted the roles to become reversed. He forgot he was given dominion over everything in the garden. He ate because he saw no physical change in Eve after she ate. He did not know the dying was a spiritual detachment from God and himself. After she ate and nothing happened to her. Adam **willfully chose to disobey God** thus committing his first act of unrighteousness. This unrighteousness is sin (to knowingly violate a divine law); as a result, he traded the truth for a lie, life for death, prosperity for knowledge, and fullness for emptiness (lack or void). Sin always has a foundational cause and leaves lasting effects. The Devil deceived

Adam and Eve by perverting or twisting God's word so they would believe a lie instead of the truth (Rom. 1:16-31 key verses 21, 23-25; Isa. 44:1-28, key verse 20; Jer. 10:14-16, 18-25).

Prior to the fall Adam and Eve were covered spiritually; although, they were physically naked. There was no sin, shame, fear, or guilt in them. After the fall, they became spiritually uncovered thus feeling the need to cover the physical body. This opens the door for man's mind to dwell in self-consciousness instead of his God ordained right to dwell in God's consciousness. This self-consciousness gives man the desire to act independently of God. They lost the power of obedience, to do only good and gained the power of disobedience to do evil. This mentally confused Adam and the manifestation distorted man's image of self. Remember prior to disobeying Adam dealt with God through the purified mind and face to face in all His splendor and truth. He now deals with God through self-consciousness and experience. Experience is knowledge or skilled acquired through being exposed to, involved in, or affected by something. This experience is based on his encounter with the Devil and eating of the fruit to know good and evil. He acquired knowledge through the senses and not through abstract reasoning of the law. After acquiring this knowledge, it contradicted his image of sinlessness and innocence along with the power to do only good as God does. Adam eyes are open now and he experiences the immediate effects of sin, which is death.

Gen. 3:7, *And the eyes of them both were opened, and they knew that they were naked; and they sewed fig leaves together, and made themselves aprons.* Whenever sin abounds, judgment comes. It can come in different forms, immediate or long suffering. God has to judge sin or He would break His Word. Adam's response indicated he didn't take responsibility for his actions. He no longer knew eternal life. He (God) placed a penalty on mankind and a savior was needed to reconcile man back to God. Therefore, neither evil nor sin can be in the presence of God, so Adam now had to hide from his Father and Creator. The covering of the body with fig leaves was a metaphor, in actuality they were trying to cover or hide their spirit and sinful soul. Their mind and heart were far from God.

Now, if you go back and examine the scripture closely, the tree was of good and evil. Evil is the failure of rational and free beings to conform in character and conduct to the will of God. The Devil interchanged the word evil for the word bad. This word bad is an attack of our true nature and character. It also disputes God's Word that everything He made was good (Gen. 1:1-31). His tactic is to make you feel you are bad so you think God doesn't love you anymore. The Devil wants you to feel there is no redemption or forgiveness to free us from these bad feelings. This will create feelings of rejection. Rejection will cause isolation as we saw with Adam, when he hid from God. It was not until man ate from the tree that he came to know evil. Eve was not given the command, so when she ate, nothing happened. It wasn't until Adam ate that man's mind was seduced and tricked by the enemy. Not only was he introduced to evil, but also guilt and shame. I am here to tell you that anything, less than God's image, is a lie, and it is implanted by the father of all lies and deception, the Devil. Therefore, the question becomes why the Devil would distort our holy image. Why would he trick us? Why does he hate us so?

The answer is jealousy, he could never occupy our place and position in God.

When the devil was put out of heaven, he lost his relationship with God along with his authority. Every since then he has been after man's relationship with God and others. His desire is to destroy: man's love for God; man's communion with God; and man's authority and dominion given by God. His jealousy seeks to destroy man's authority by way of mind seduction and control. He is constantly seeking ways to attack the head of every nation, country, state, city, town, church and family. When you remove the "(d)" from Devil the word becomes "evil". His true character is evil and he enjoys sharing it.

Conclusion: Relationship of Disobedience.
1. Conquer you by seduction and deception of the mind.
2. Defy God, His Word and His plan.

2ND ALTAR CONFESSION OF FAITH

PURPOSE: SEEK HIS STANDARD

JORDAN means VALLEY
JOSHUA 1:10, 3:5

Make Preparation and Sanctify Yourself

Joshua stepped on the stones. After Jacob's encounter with God at the first altar, the rock is reduced to stones. What seemed huge and insurmountable is now conquered through Jesus Christ. Joshua is required in Matthew 11:28-30 to: *Come to Me, all you who labor and are heavy-laden and overburdened, and I will cause you to rest. [I will ease and relieve and refresh your souls.] Take my yoke upon you, and learn of Me, for I am gentle (meek) and humble (lowly) in heart, and you will find rest (relief and ease and refreshment and recreation and blessed quiet) for your souls [Jer. 6:16]. For my yoke is wholesome (useful, good—not harsh, hard, sharp, or pressing, but comfortable, gracious, and pleasant), and My burden is light and easy to be borne.*

Here stepping on the stones denotes his struggle and wrestling were over. He can trust God to lead and provide for him. Stepping on the stone is a metaphor: in actuality, he is stepping on Jesus because at this altar, sanctification is impossible without Him. Changing into His image is the goal.

Altar of

Sanctification cleansing by water baptism.

Surrenders-trust in Him.

Obedience-learning responsibility for self.

This altar defines God's:

1. Purpose for your life.

2. Plan for your destiny.

Discover who God wants you to be!

Water Sanctification-Outer and inner man delivered from outside influences. Sin always destroys whatever it touches. Unless stopped, sin is always progressive.

The brazen laver was the bowl where the priests washed and cleansed themselves. Therefore, this altar is the removal of our old fleshly nature through the washing of the water by the Word. This is a place where you are washed and purged from former behaviors, strongholds and unholy desires (Romans 8:5-13).

Test: There is a continuation of testing, so God may have His perfect work in you. I am not concerned about others but about making a choice to change self. If others never change, I will be transformed.

Trial: The challenge here is to step out of your circle of friends, and step into God's will for your life. Your surrendering and obedience to walk circumspectly according to God's Word and His divine purpose will bring great glory to Him. Others will see the great transformation in your life; thus, opening the door for them to be won to Christ.

CHANGE YOUR PLAN!
Change My Standards

Joshua did not use the old plan; he didn't imitate Moses' style. He chose to be himself. He compromised on the method, but not his convictions or principles. He was decisive and committed to his destiny. God granted inner and outer peace and security to him.

You are sanctified from Carnality.

At this altar, three key elements are presented: sanctification, surrendering, and obedience.

1. Sanctification-There was specific instructions given to Israel. Passing through the water represented water baptism (an outward sign of cleansing).

A. Wash thoroughly (Ps. 51:2).

B. Purge yourself with hyssop (Ps. 51:7)

C. Lay aside every weight (Heb. 12:1).

Our text tells them to sanctify themselves because God can only do what we allow Him to do. This leads us to step two.

2. Surrendering represented the act of yielding; submission; giving up control. Stepping on the stones was to show forth their trust in God. They trusted that they would not die while passing through the process of burial. For God would resurrect them at the next altar. This surrendering permits the believers to yield their members and rebirth unto holiness and righteousness.

3. Obedience-To pick up the stones meant they had to bend over which represented a humbling of self in direct obedience to God. Be responsible for yourself. This is an individual walk and relationship. You know where you are. I am here now, but I was back there. Picking the stones up was a reminder that I have changed. Also carrying the stones was to denote He was with them and no burden was too hard for Him to fix. God is calling you into obedience to Him and His Word. Cut off the works of the flesh. The Devil does not control us anymore … Greater is he that is in you, than he that is the world (I John 4:4). Sanctification, surrendering and obedience permit the Christian to walk in the spirit and handle any outer obstacle without.

Let's examine these three areas more thoroughly: sanctification, surrendering and obedience. Our text **Joshua 3:5** states, And Joshua said to the people, "Sanctify yourselves, for tomorrow the Lord will do wonders among you." Here Joshua is telling the people to sanctify themselves because God has made us free-will agents and He can only do what we ask Him to do in us. In addition, a key point in this verse is made, after sanctification God showed himself mightily on their behalf. We want the wonders without the sanctification and sacrifices. We want to accept God without forsaking the world. Heaven is a prepared place for a prepared people. You will not tip toe through the tulips at this altar. This altar requires you to work, you know what needs cleaning. This altar prepares you to move to the third altar.

What Is Sanctification?

Sanctification (Gk.) hagiasmos, separation, a setting apart, to be holy. In the Old Testament, it denotes the consecration of a person to God (Ex. 31:13). To make holy or to set apart for God (Gen 2:3); consecration; a separation unto God from a profane secular world.

In the New Testament, the doctrine is making truly perfectly holy what was defiled and sinful, and is a progressive work of divine grace upon the soul justified by the love of Christ. After a gradual cleansing from sin the sinner presented " unspotted before the throne of God," which is the work of the Holy Spirit. The ultimate sanctification of every believer in Christ is a covenant of mercy, purchased on the cross[4].

In the old and new testament, men are called upon to sanctify themselves, to consecrate themselves truly to God (Ex. 19:22; Lev. 11:44; 20:7-8: I Pet. 3:15). We have become very lazy and abusive with the grace of God. We use grace as a gastric by past. We look for bootleg surgeons (preachers) who will lay hands upon us and who will co-sign our failure and non-commitment to God to live holy. You should realize by now sanctification is setting oneself apart from evil and dedicating oneself to God.

This sanctification is done by washing and purging oneself of unrighteousness. In Joshua 3:14-17: The priest entered the water before the people. They were the only ones to get their feet wet. This was a metaphor

---

4   Smiths Bible Dictionary p. 267 (def.) sanctification

of the New Testament feet washing. It was one man from each of the twelve tribes, which represents the twelve disciples. The wetting of the feet was Jesus' way of washing their feet. I believe he used the priest to remind them that God was calling them to servitude and humility. This servitude was selfless love which He continued to show Israel.

After the priest stepped into the water, it began to dry up. This miracle was performed because Israel's sanctification called forth God's awesome power to work on their behalf. The people were told to pass through. Passing through the water was a representation of New Testament water baptism. Baptism is the application of water as a rite of purification or initiation; a Christian sacrament. The word baptism is the English for the Gk. Baptismos. The verb from which this noun is derived— baptizo means to dip, immerse or submerge. The Old Testament baptism was water purification, which symbolized cleansing of a person or object. The New Testament Christian baptism is a testimony that pictures the death, and resurrection of Christ. By participating in this external rite, the believer professes his death to sin and resurrection to spiritual life (Rom 6:3-5; Gal

3:27 Col. 3:3). Therefore under the New Testament to be sanctified these elements must exist: the Spirit (is what draws you); the Word (is what cleanses you), the altar (is where he was sacrificed), the blood of Jesus (is what paid for our penalty) and our faith (is what makes it possible). In II Thess. 2:13...God hath from the beginning chosen you to salvation through sanctification of the Spirit and belief of the truth. Here, as a New Testament Christian we are required to have more than just water purification, we must cleanse ourselves from all unrighteousness. We must wash thoroughly (Isaiah 1:16-18) and ask God to purge us from all unrighteousness (Psalm 51:1-9).

What is Surrendering?

Surrendering is letting go and letting God have His way. It is trusting in God and His plan. We must learn to lay aside every weight and sin that so easily beset us. We must release ourselves into God's new lifestyle for us. The bible clearly commands believers to surrender to God, obey His Word and submit to His will. Jesus asked that the cup be removed from Him, but He trusted and surrendered to God; therefore, He stated, "...Not my will, but thine, be done (Luke 22:42). At the end of His life's earthly suit, He cried, "My God My God why have you Forsaken Me, yet He trusted to commend His spirit back into His father's hand (Mark. 15:34; Luke 23:46). The cross signifies Jesus' total surrendering to the will of God. In the resurrection, He is raised from the dead and exalted to Heaven. He shows the correlation of obedience has to a blessing. After being obedient to the cross, He was resurrected and sits on the right hand side of God, the Father (Mk. 16:19). No matter what the price or outcome, He trusted in God.

Finally, we must deal with obedience, the very act of listening and doing His will. Every victory of Israel was based on her obedience to God. This also holds true for us today. We must always learn to obey God's Word (Duet. 4:30-31; 11:1-32; Dan. 7:27; Acts 5:29). We are required to hear His Word and do His will (James 1:22). We must listen to the instructions given by His Spirit or Word. We try the Spirit by the Word of God to call forth its authenticity. We must submit and say yes to God. We release all our desires and desire what God wants. Our obedience is to flow out of love for God (I John 2:3-5).

If we love the Lord, we will want to serve Him; and in serving Him, we will want to obey His commandments. Acts of obedience, therefore, are to be reflective of an inner reality that we love the Lord deeply and are committed to Him completely. Obedience is not an automatic response. It must be learned.

Although Israel won many victories she also suffered many penalties because of her disobedience to God (Jer. 7:13; Hos. 9:17). The Lord offers undeserved mercy, grace and forgiveness to those who confess their disobedience and make a new choice to obey (Rom. 11:30-32).

This altar is an altar of responsibility. It demands self-evaluation. Many times we are waiting for some one else to fix us. We are looking for the Pastor to wave a magic wand so all our problems will disappear. Well, I am here to tell you, it does not work like that. Many of us have spent years tricking up our lives and we want an instant fix. Neither God nor the Pastor is a drug dealers. They do not sell drugs that will give you a temporary solution to a long-term problem. The Pastor is the shepherd who watches over your soul, not the repairer of it.

The only way your soul can be renewed and repaired is through seeking Jesus Christ. We expect some type of genie to make us brand new. God is not your man and He is not looking for a prostitute. Therefore, you cannot manipulate Him with your tricks or your treats. He doesn't do Halloween; He is not a nightmare on Elm Street. So, if you looking for Freddy Cougar, Chuckie, Boo or any of the other gang, you have the wrong number. Try again because this connection will never go through. He is looking for honesty; He already knows where you are. When Adam and Eve decided they would hide their nakedness behind fig leaves, God commanded their presence by asking: "Where Art Thou?" Many are hiding in the pew slipping and sliding, but God knows right where you are. He is waiting for you to recognize it and ask for help.

We are looking for someone else to seek God's will for us. Work out your own soul salvation (Phil. 2:12-13). You are a unique human being and each one has a divine purpose and calling. You are here on earth for a specific reason that is full of destiny.

We are seeking someone else to pray and fast. The people kept asking the Pastor to pray for them. His response was pray for yourself; my tongue is tired. You know you and your crazy peeps (family) have worn him out. Ha Ha! The question I would ask you are how many hours have you prayed about a problem? Do not ask any one else to pray for something which you will not labor in prayer for yourself. Grow up and demand others to grow up around you. This altar requires growth. When I was a child, I talked like a child, I thought like a child, I reasoned like a child; now that I have become a man, I am done with childish ways and have put them aside (I Cor. 13:11 AMP). Concerning this we have much to say which is hard to explain, since you have become dull in your [spiritual] hearing and sluggish [even slothful in achieving spiritual insight]. For even though by this time you ought to be teaching others, you actually need someone to teach you over again the very first principles of God's Word. You have come to need milk, not solid food. For everyone who continues to feed on milk is obviously inexperienced and unskilled in the doctrine of righteousness (of conformity to the divine will in purpose, thought, and action), for he is a mere infant [not able to talk yet]! But solid food is for full-grown men, for those whose senses and mental faculties are trained by practice to discriminate and distinguish between what is morally good and noble and what is evil and contrary either to divine or human law (Heb. 5:11-14 AMP).

We want someone else to step into the water for us. You know we have many excuses why we cannot sanctify ourselves. However, Jesus came to the pool of Bethesda and asked the man will he be made whole. The man began to make excuses, he stated when the water is troubled I have no one to assist me. Then he said, the people always step in before me. He finally told him, I did not ask you all that I asked would you be made whole (John 5:1-9). So I ask you if not now, when?

We want someone else to take up the stones. To take up the stones required hard work. If a stone is embedded in dirt and you decide to remove it, the first thing you must do is begin to dig around the stone. Many times, it is larger than what the physical eye can see and other materials (grass, vines, glass, mold etc.) wrap itself around the stone. Next, you must separate whatever has attached itself to the stone. Afterwards you must dig under the stone while prying it away from the soil. Finally, you must lift it out of the soil. This is the same process we must go through in order to be changed. We must go through a surgery, which detaches and separates us from the unclean things, along with recovery, which regenerates or renews the inner man.

To pick up the stones, the priest had to bow. He had to bend over which represent a humbling of self in direct obedience of God. Picking up and carrying the stones with them were to show them that God was to go everywhere they went. It also let Israel know that they would not die in the valley while passing through altar one and two, but would be resurrected at the next altar.

We are looking for someone else to discipline our flesh. You must serve notice to this body that it will transform itself. You must serve eviction papers and remove the old tenant before you can enter into a new contract or covenant. At the altar God is saying flee or run from fornication. What is fornication here? It is all the old habits you keep continuing. All the old partners with whom you keep sleeping; overeating, lack of budgeting, selfishness, filthy thoughts etc. We are looking for someone else to stop our bad habits. Some people would rather have a gastric by pass than to back up from the table. It takes twenty-one consecutive days to start a new habit. Will you dedicate yourself to changing you? If you won't, who will?

Here God is calling you to examine and adjust yourself. In the old days, we had ovens you had to clean yourself by scouring and scraping the residue off the walls. Today we have self-cleaning ovens that require the oven to do the work itself and all you have to do is wipe the walls clean. God is saying go back to the old landmark. Where there was no question about how to get clean. There is no such thing as setting a knob to clean you. The only tool that cleans you is the Word of God. So get in the Word and deal with this temple (body, soul and spirit) by purging and disciplining the flesh.

Repent: Wash yourselves, make yourselves clean; put away the evil of your doings from before My eyes! Cease to do evil, Learn to do right! Seek justice, relieve the oppressed, and correct the oppressor. Defend the fatherless, plead for the widow. Come now, and let us reason together, says the Lord. Though your sins are like scarlet, they shall be as white as snow; though they are red like crimson, they shall be like wool. If you are willing and obedient, you shall eat the good of the land; but if you refuse and rebel, you will be devoured by the sword. For the mouth of the Lord has spoken it (Isa. 1:16-20).

Pray: Come aside and sup with me (Jesus Christ). Come seeking God so He can commune with you and download His will into your life. Start praying for divine intervention and release.

Fast: Start denying the flesh the external pleasures it seeks to enjoy. Make it obey God, and teach it discipline, so you will not fulfill the lust of the flesh.

Study: Begin to read God's word and establish a personal study time.

In Joshua 3:5 they were told to sanctify themselves. Let us see what the scripture says about coming into this new way. Read Galatians 5:1-26. God is calling us to righteousness and holiness (Lev. 19, I Peter 1:13-20). Holiness is a lifestyle; it is separating oneself from anything impure or unclean. It sets one apart from sin and immoral living. And that ye put on the new man, which after God is created in righteousness and true holiness (Ephesians 4:24). In living in holiness and righteousness before him, all the days of our life (Luke 1:75).

Romans 6:18-22 AMP states: And having been set free from sin, you have become the servants of righteousness (of conformity to the divine will in thought, purpose and action). I am speaking in familiar human terms because of your natural limitations. For as you yielded your bodily members [and faculties] as servants to impurity and ever increasing lawlessness, so now yield your bodily members [and faculties] once for all as servants to righteousness (right being and doings) [which leads] to sanctification. For when you were slaves of sin, you were free in regard to righteousness. But then what benefit (return) did you get from the things of which you are now ashamed? [None] for the end of those things is death. But now since you have been set free from sin and have become the slaves of God, you have your present reward in holiness and its end is eternal life. In His Word are standards by which He has called us to follow, so we may get cleansed and remain cleansed.

You are married to God or the Devil! No man can serve two masters. There is no middle ground. God does not want you to be lukewarm for he will spew you out of his mouth (Rev. 3:16). Make a choice! Ye cannot drink the cup of the Lord, and the cup of devils: ye cannot be partakers of the Lord's table, and of the table of devils (I Corinthians 10:21). Woe to those who call evil good and good evil, who put darkness for light and light for darkness, who put bitter for sweet and sweet for bitter (Isaiah 5:20 NKJV).

I appeal to you therefore, brethren, and beg of you in view of [all] the mercies of God, to make a decisive dedication of your bodies [presenting all your members and faculties] as a living sacrifice, holy (devoted, consecrated) and well pleasing to God, which is your reasonable (rational, intelligent) service and spiritual worship. Do not be conformed to this world (this age), [fashioned after and adapted to its external, superficial customs], but be transformed (changed) by the [entire] renewal of your mind [by its new ideals and its new attitude], so that you may prove [for yourselves] what is good and acceptable and perfect will of God, even the thing which is good and acceptable and perfect [in His sight for you] (Romans 12:1-2 AMP). We no longer set before God animal sacrifice on the altar, but we become living sacrifices through the redemptive blood of Jesus Christ.

James asks us to prepare ourselves with self-control, self-denial, abstinence and mortification. Therewith bless we God, even the Father; and therewith curse we men, which are made after the similitude of God. Out of the same mouth proceeded blessing and cursing. My brethren, these things ought not so to be. Doth a fountain send forth at the same place sweet water and bitter? Can the fig tree, my brethren, bear olives berries? either a vine, figs? so can no fountain both yield salt water and fresh? (James 3:9-12). James is admonishing us to take control of the flesh bring it subject to one direction of good or evil. A double minded man is unstable in all his ways (Jas. 1:8; 4:8). He also urges us to kill or mortify our flesh. So kill (deaden, deprive of power) the evil desire lurking in your members [those animal impulses and all that is earthly in you that is employed in sin]: sexual vice, impurity, sensual appetites, unholy desires, and all greed and covetousness, for that is idolatry (the deifying of self and other created things instead of God). It is on account of these [very sins] that the [holy] anger of God is ever coming upon the sons of disobedience (those who are obstinately opposed to the divine will). Among whom you also once walked, when you were living in and addicted to [such practices]. But now put away and rid yourselves [completely] of all these things: anger, rage, bad feeling toward others, curses and slander, and foulmouthed abuse and shameful utterances from your lips! Do not lie to one another, for you have stripped off the old (unregenerate) self with its evil practices, And have clothed yourselves with the new [spiritual self], which is [ever in the process of being] renewed and remolded into [fuller and more perfect knowledge upon] knowledge after the image (the likeness) of Him Who created it (Col. 3:5-10 AMP).

What preparation must we make for ourselves? Romans 13:12-14 NKJVstates: The night is far spent, the day is at hand. Therefore let us cast off the works of darkness, and let us put on the armor of light. Let us walk properly, as in the day, not in revelry and drunkenness, not in lewdness and lust, not in strife and envy. But put on the Lord Jesus Christ, and make no provision for the flesh, to fulfill its lusts. Here the Apostle Paul is talking to Christians, not the sinners. Here the Christians were hanging onto past sins. You are sanctifying yourself against the Devil's playground, which is the works of the flesh: the works of the Devil are sin, sickness, fear, death, depression, murder, temptation, deception lust and rebellion (Eph. 4:27, Gal. 5:19-26 NKJV).

Read Romans Chapter 8: Paul let us know that Christ made it possible to cease walking after the flesh, and equipped us with power to walk in the spirit so we will not fulfill the lust of the flesh. We are no longer debtors to sin, but to Jesus Christ our Lord and Savior. You can be free; your body parts do not have to be enslaved to the past or mischief.

Conclusion: Relationship of Sanctification, change of body.

1. Spiritual man cleansed.

2. Flesh brought under subjection.

   a. The flesh is taught to surrender and obey.

2ND BAAL ALTAR
SUBTLE BODY CONTROL

PURPOSE: ENSLAVEMENT OF THE FLESH THROUGH CARNALITY

At this altar, the Devil chooses to control the body. The goal is to bring an imbalance of the spiritual and carnal man. The word carnality comes from the Greek word Sarkikos, which when translated into English connotes "rotten" flesh. Carnality is anti-spiritual in nature, and appeals to the appetite of the soul. He wants the believer to starve and weaken the spirit, thus, empowering the flesh with the temptation of sin. The carnal man is drawn away from God with lust (James 1:13-15, 4:1-6).

Lusts (works of the flesh) def. evil desires which readily express themselves in bodily activities. They are "natural tendencies" of the flesh and soulish capacity and proclivity to gravitate toward things that are evil.

Desire, in itself is not to be feared. God gives us the desires of our hearts (Ps. 37:4). Lust, however, is perverted desire which leads to sin. When lust prevails in our lives, we may get what we want, but we will lose what we have (Num. 11:4-5, 31-34; Rom. 1:27). What looks desirable and good are things that will put you into bondage.

At this altar the devil centers things on feelings. He creates temporarily good feelings that have harmful life altering effects. These things become terrible habits and eventually turn into addictions, spiraling downward to sin and iniquity.

Altar of

Rejection of the truth and principles.

Rebellion against the Word of God.

Uncleanliness through lack of discipline.

This altar seeks

1. Control of the body through:

a. lust of the eye; b. lust of the flesh; c. pride of life (I John 2:16).

2. Control of the flesh through evil habits.

1. Control of the body: a. lust of the eye (Matt. 5:28; Rom. 7:7; I Cor. 10:6-10). Our eye must be centered on Christ. It demands a singleness centering only on Christ. It is a doorway for sin to enter our spirits. When our eyes drift away from Christ, it permits lust to pervert and captivate it. We begin to covet what is not ours (Ex. 20:17).

b. lust of the flesh (Rom. 6:12, 8:5-8, 7:24, 13:14; Gal. 5:16-17, 19-21; Eph 4:29-5:5). The flesh is controlled by the mind and since the Devil deceived you at the first altar, the body begins to act according to the information received and partake in ungodly desires.

c. pride of life (Col. 2:18). One of the things that precede pride is anger. When anger is unchecked (Eph. 4:26, 27, 31) and fueled by pride it will reject God's will in order to cling to its own will or way. This altar rejects and rebels against God's truth, principles and Word. When this happens, man is confronted with **PMS**. They will deal with this always. Whenever a man falls, it will be because of **POWER**, **MONEY**, and or **SEX**, which is a result of the lust of the eye, lust of the flesh and the pride of life. Why do men seek power? Since man was put out the garden, he has sought after power. Money, itself, is not evil. It is the love of money, by humanity, in which the danger lies within (I Tim. 6:9-10). Sex is to be exercised under the marriage covenant between two legally married (state registered documents) consenting adults. It was designed for two purposes: First, it consummates (spiritually binds the two together) the marriage by the intertwining or joining the two individuals into one flesh by means of sexual intercourse. The virgin bride's hymen is broken and a blood covenant and soul tie is made, giving the partner rights and privileges for life. There is no such thing as casual sex. Second for procreation, it was designed to give offspring through reproduction, another tie to this individual for life. Now we can look everywhere and see how the marriage bed is compromised and defiled by adultery and fornication.

2. Control of the flesh through evil habits (James 1:13-16; 4:1-6 Gal. 5:16-19). We give the enemy permission to enter and control our flesh when "we are drawn away by our own lust." Since we rejected and rebelled against God's truth and principles, our core beliefs and motives will be fueled by an impure selfish will and desire. If they are driven by contaminated thoughts, we will

forsake all morals and values. At this point, the sin is interpreted as missing the mark. What appears desirable and good are mere illusions created by the Devil that will entice and captivate you into life long bondages of sin. The system of power, money and sex becomes fleshly obsessions, empowers the carnal mind, and increases our sinful appetite. Power, money or sex, in itself is not evil, it is the content of which it is utilized and practiced. Throughout this book you will see how the Devil constantly told man that he needs more power to dominate the earth; so he can become independent of God; how many men have sold their souls for mere mortal crumbs of money that will never reach eternity; how he continually uses sexual seduction to entice Israel and today's humanity into immorality and idolatry.

This altar defies the purity and holiness of Christianity. Israel was a holy and chosen people, a royal priesthood, a royal diadem called out to serve a Holy God (Deut 7:6-11; I Pet 2:9). It also defies and denounces the Ten Commandments given to Israel, which we are to keep today. In Exodus 20:1-6 states: "And God spake all these words, saying, I am the Lord thy God, which brought thee out of the land of Egypt, out of the house of bondage. Thou shalt have no other gods before me. Thou shalt not make unto thee any graven image, or any likeness of any thing that is in heaven above, or that is in the earth beneath, or that is in the water under the earth: Thou shalt not bow down thyself to them, nor serve them: for I the Lord thy God am a jealous God, visiting the iniquity of the fathers upon the children unto the third and fourth generation of them that hate me; And shewing mercy unto thousands of them that love me, and keep my commandments…"

God warned Israel of the danger of interracial marriage because He knew it would dilute their love, faith, pure worship and obedience to Him the true and living God. This would destroy their morality and sanctification. "When the Lord your God brings you into the land which you go to possess, and has cast out many nations before you, the Hittites and the Girgashites and the Amorites and the Canaanites and the Perizzites and the Hivites and the Jebusites, seven nations greater and mightier than you, and when the Lord your God delivers them over to you, you shall conquer them and utterly destroy them. You shall make no covenant with them nor show mercy to them. Nor shall you make marriages with them. You shall not give your daughter to their son, nor take their daughter for your son. For they will turn your sons away from following Me, to serve other gods; so the anger of the Lord will be aroused against you and destroy you suddenly. But thus you shall deal with them: you shall destroy their altars, and break down their sacred pillars, and cut down their wooden images, and burn them with fire" (Duet 7:1-5 NKJV). Marriage unites two people as one in spirit, mind and flesh. Many of the heathens owned land, and were merchants; so, many of these marriages to foreigners, were based on economical and social status, and not love. Since Israel didn't do as they were told and chose to intermingle with the heathens, they brought among them idol gods.

Below are some of their gods they worshipped.

The Moon God: The false god at work is Ashtaroth. This is the name of the Canaanites' principle female deity (Judges 2:11-13) which was to be embodied in the moon. This idol was of female descent with a crescent moon on her eyebrow. This idol was in the temples and worshipped with the most revolting forms of immorality or sexual perversion. This form of worship hid under the name religion, and all righteous virtue and decency was lost.[5]

The Asherah was another idol worshipped at this altar as the tree of life. The word asherah comes from the root ashar, to be straight; upright, erected. It was made out of tree poles and were symbols of the phallus and represented procreation. The pillar was set upright in the ground. The Canaanites and other pagans used this form of worship (Judges 2:13, 10:6). These objects were placed outside the temple for perverse worshipping. This is how the corrupt priesthood of idol gods made their living, and is practiced still today in many pagan countries. The people participated in demoralizing and demonizing obscene orgies (Ex. 34:15, Judges 2:17). Here at this altar all decency and virtue is surrendered and the flesh takes control. In addition, it perverts all members of the flesh into unrighteousness and unseemliness. Satisfaction is never achieved and the body craves and desires more. The heart is hardened to the things of God and heart surgery or heart circumcision is needed at the next altar.[6]

---

[5] The Dake Annotated Reference Bible KJV, p. 452 letter y.

---

[6] The Dake Annotated Reference Bible KJV, p. 194 Asherah.

The spirits are in operation at this altar: The spirit of jealousy, lying spirit, perverse spirit, spirit of haughtiness, spirit of heaviness, and the spirit of whoredom. In the old days, you laid on the altar to bring the flesh under subjection and into obedience to God. You lay on the altar until you were ready and able to release yourself from these strongholds. The saints of yesterday knew you had to wash, purge and mortify the members of the flesh, which released you from corruption.

In each story below, you will find PMS (power, money or sex) tempting mankind. Most of them will fall due to fleshly desires. Today so many of our men are powerless and undisciplined in the area of bringing the flesh under subjection. Each man has the power of choice to decide will he bow to Baal or will he stand for God.

In Exodus 34:12-17 the laws were renewed among Israel: "Take heed to thyself, lest thou make a covenant with the inhabitants of the land whither thou goest, lest it be for snare in the midst of thee: But ye shall destroy their altars, break their images, and cut down their groves: For thou shalt worship no other god: for the Lord, whose name is Jealous, is a jealous God. Lest thou make a covenant with the inhabitants of the land, and they go a whoring after their gods (devils), and do sacrifice unto their gods, and one call thee, and thou eat of his sacrifice; And thou take of their daughters unto thy sons, and their daughters go a whoring after their gods (false gods), and make thy sons go a whoring after their gods. Thou shalt make thee no molten gods."

In this text below, Samson and his family knew this law and his parents lightly forewarned him of his disobedience to the law. I have shown above three different scriptural references (Ex. 20:1-6; Duet. 7:1-5; Ex. 34:12-17), with which Samson was taught and consciously disobeyed God's explicit command not to intermarry with heathens. He also neglected his calling and ministry. Samson's mother had a problem with the curse of barrenness, (found in the first Baal altar under seed reproduction), but God chose to bless her with a child. This blessing came with conditions, *"For, lo, thou shalt conceive, and bear a son; and no razor shall come on his head: for the child shall be a Nazarite unto God from the womb: and he shall begin to deliver Israel out of the hand of the Philistines (Judges 13:5).* The word Nazarite comes from nazir meaning consecrated. The unshaven hair of a Nazarite was a sign of his consecration, sanctification and dedication to God. It also signified his strength and power to the service of God. A Nazarite was commanded: not to drink any wine or strong drink, no vinegar of wine, no vinegar of strong drink, no liquor of grapes, eat no ripe grapes or dried grapes, eat nothing from the vine tree or kernels of the husk, no razor was to come upon his head; for he shall be holy, he shall not make himself uncleaned or defiled (Num. 6:1-7).

You will see Samson's biggest challenge was dealing with his power and sexual immorality. Samson chose to lie with Delilah: In Judges chapters 13-15 you will find the life story of Samson the Nazarene. Samson was one of the Judges over Israel; he was chosen and called for the deliverance of them. You will see how Samson rebelled and rejected against God's truth and His principles. As a Nazarene, he was to abstain from strong drink and not touch or eat anything unclean. Samson overstepped his boundary by choosing his own wife; according to the law, his father Manoah was to pick his wife. Again, I will reiterate how Samson's parents tried to remind him to find a woman of his own tribe, but he did not listen (Jud. 14:3). You will find he kept playing with fire until he was burned. Delilah was a vessel who permitted the Devil to use her to deceive the man of God. Samson struggled with the weakness of sexual impurity. He loved foreign women, which served idol gods. He had three women in his life and each one was a Philistine. Samson's wife from Timnath (14:1-4); the harlot in Gath (16:1-3); and Delilah of Sorek (16:4-25). Samson found a woman whose family was his enemy and hated him or because of another woman whom he loved. Samson fell deeply in love with these women, who caused others to take advantage of him by deception and trickery. Five of the leaders of the Philistine promised Delilah eleven hundred pieces of silver if she could give them the secret to Samson's power. Quite naturally, the leaders were jealous of his strength and wanted to kill him. We see the spirit of jealousy at work. Samson lied to Delilah three times but she kept seducing him until he uncovers the secret of his success. The deceiver was deceived and the seducer was seduced. This deception amused him; he entertained and chose to invite the lying spirit in (16: 7-14). Each time Delilah tried to capture Samson and failed, he let his pride elevate and engage with the spirit of haughtiness. Samson played with Delilah until she discovered the secret to his success (16: 15-17).

In this sexual soul tie (intercourse) was where he uncovered his heart. Where your heart is, so are your treasures. His inner heart was a place where only God and he belonged.

No other person (no parent, child, lover etc.), place or things are supposed to occupy this space. When we allow others in this special sacred place, all they can do is break our heart, wound our spirit and weary our soul. Many times, it is hard to pick up the pieces and move on or return to God. God never intended for things (objects) to enter the heart. They have no spirit to commune with nor do they house love. Things are benefits given by God to enhance our lifestyle.

However, Samson decided to let a perverted devil (a god of a foreign spirit) penetrate his spirit. If we examine these chapters closely, you will see the spirit of whoredom in the natural (adultery of the flesh) and spirit (adultery of the spirit) realm at work. The spirit houses the heart and emotions, and it is our job to guard and protect them. Don't give the devil any ground; don't entertain him not even for a moment. Samson's strength did not lie in his hair or in his muscles but in his relationship and faith he had with God and the spirit of the Lord (Jud. 13:24-25, 14:6, 19, 15:14). His hair was a token of his vow to God and represented the relationship with Him that gave him strength. His hair, which never to be cut, was a metaphor of his relationship with

God that would never cease. Samson recognized he had committed spiritual adultery and was in a backslidden condition. Today we expect restoration without repentance. He repented and spiritually woke up from carnality and sin; he lost his life but not his soul.

In each of these stories listed below, you will see the second altar spirits at work: jealousy, lying, perverse, haughtiness, heaviness and whoredom.

When the devil tempted Jesus, he used the system of power: "Then was Jesus led up of the Spirit into the wilderness to be tempted of the devil. And when he had fasted forty days and forty nights, he was afterward a hungred. And when the tempter came to him, he said, "<u>If</u> thou be the Son of God, command that these stones be made of bread. But he answered and said, *It is written, Man shall not live by bread alone, but by every word that proceedeth out of the mouth of God.* Then the devil taketh him up into the holy city, and setteth him on a pinnacle of the temple, And saith unto him, <u>If</u> thou be the Son of God, cast thyself down: for it is written, He shall give his angels charge concerning thee: and in their hands they shall bear thee up, lest any time thou dash thy foot against a stone. Jesus said unto him, *It is written again, Thou shalt not tempt the Lord thy God.* Again, the devil taketh him up into an exceeding high mountain, and sheweth him all the kingdoms of the world, and the glory of them; And saith unto him, All these things will I give thee; If thou wilt fall down and worship me. Then saith Jesus unto him, *Get thee hence, Satan: for it is written, Thou shalt worship the Lord thy God, and him only shalt serve thou serve"* (Matt. 4:1-11). When the Devil comes to tempt, the first thing he introduces is doubt. Therefore, he tried to get Jesus to doubt the Word of God, he tempted His flesh, His character and His dominion. When Jesus stood His ground and only answered with the Word, he moves on. Since he can't conquer the Word, he went to the next subject. In Genesis Eve entertained the Devil, Jesus resisted the Devil by just quoting the Word and that is what we must do. Jesus refused to submit or bow to the Devil or His flesh. He knew who He was and His birthright couldn't be bought. He refused to sell or submit Himself for food or money as Esau and Judas. Satan will tempt those who are heavily anointed to do God's will, but we must oppose and overcome all temptation.

When Judas was tempted and deceived by the Devil, he was tempted with money. He was so connected to a system; he betrayed Jesus, took his life, and sentenced himself to hell by committing suicide (Matt. 26:1-25; 27:3-9).

Ananias and Sapphira choose to sell all their possessions and give the funds to the church. When they gave the church the money, they lied to the disciples and the Holy Spirit about the amount. They were so tied to this system of money that they lied and died (Acts 5:1-10). You cannot compromise the spirit of truth (Holy Spirit) with the spirit of the deceiver (Devil). Will you rob God or are you faithful with your tithes and offering?

King David was tempted through the system of power and sex, when he desired Uriah's wife Bathsheba. His desire for her turned into lust. He committed adultery and she became pregnant. His goal was to cover up the pregnancy by having her husband sleep with her. When that didn't work he had Uriah killed. David was cursed and penalized for his act of sin and disobedience. His first child died at birth. (II Samuel 11 and 12). This system of sex destroyed many of his children's lives. He was unable to build the temple of God because his hands had blood on them. His children were affected by this sexual generational curse. I must tell you that it grew worst as it erupted in the next generation. David's son Amnon raped his stepsister Tamar, and then Absalom killed his brother (II Sam. 13-15:12). Absalom rebelled against his father and made himself king. He had sex with his father's concubine on the roof (II Sam. 15:13-19:43).

Many of our leaders are tempted through these same Systems of PMS: President Clinton defamed his position with a momentarily pleasure of oral sex; Rev. Jessie Jackson forgot his covenant and committed adultery and produced a child; Athletes are transmitting sexual diseases to their mates; Senators are having sexual relationship with pages, male and female prostitutes; Popes are assaulting male children. Mayors and Governors are being discharged for stealing money. Political, religious and business leaders are caught abusing power. I urge you as Christians and Leaders not to be caught in this web of deception. Don't think women are exempt; they, too, can be effected and fall because they abuse power, money and sex.

God is looking for a Virgin Bride (pure church) when He returns without spot or wrinkle, but the Devil's counter attack is impurity and sexual perversion. We see it everywhere today; however, this is another tactic of the enemy to weary God's people. When Christians look at religious and political leaders who lack self-control it makes them feel hopeless and powerless. This sexual perversion is only an attempt for the church to look evil. Nevertheless, I say to every born again believer, don't submit to the temptation of sexual deviant behavior. Don't fall into the trap. There is a penalty to sin even if it looks as though many got by. For the wages of sin in death; but the gift of God is eternal life through Jesus Christ our Lord (Rom. 6:23).

This perversion can be found in the pulpit. Too many Christian husbands and wives are covering up for their sinful, grace abusers and perverted mates. They are turning a deaf ear and a blinded eye to their mates continued infidelity and impurity, leaving it unexposed. These people are the shepherds; yet they act like wolves preying on the weak. Where are the honor, integrity and morality? There are many Pastors raping the young, living on the down low, having lengthy sexual affairs that are producing children. These are not oops, I slipped; they are lengthy acts of unrighteousness and iniquities. They are backslidden and still preaching in the pulpit, heading for apostasy. Many are seeking a temporary thrill, but it will produce a lifetime of gloom and doom. It is time to raise a standard in Zion and each one must act accordingly to holiness and righteousness. Do you know how hard it is to revive a soul that was wounded by an impure leader?

God severely judges sexual perversion. In II Peter 2:4-7 God would not spare the angels that, sinned, or the old world, which was flooded and only Noah and his family spared nor the cities of Sodom and Gomorrah except Lot and his family. What makes you think you will be exempt as a leader? Lot's wife was so connected to the adulterous and perverted system of Sodom and Gomorrah; when the angels told them to leave the city and don't look back, she looked and turned into a pillar of salt. I asked myself why a pillar of salt? We as the righteous are to be a beacon light on the hill and the salt of the earth. Salt is a preserver, a purifier; she was to be preserved and saved yet the sin became a soul tie, an endeavoring connection to the heart and spirit.

Therefore, she looked and was destroyed. Don't get so engulfed to this earthly realm that you are no heavenly good. Everything on this earth are benefits, lent to us by God for a season and for an appointed time. Nothing remains the same except God. Know that change is inevitable. This is the basis of God's altars that you will alter (adjust) yourself for each of them.

However, we must learn that God is God and He cannot be tempted; even when we are tempted he makes a way of escape (James 1:13). Nothing in this earth should be more valuable than our relationship with God. When they are, we make gods out of them and they obtain His space. God has given each thing to us and we should never put anything before him. That means no relationship with any human being or material thing should take us away from him. That is a grave dishonor and disrespect for Him. "Have no other gods before Him" (Ex. 20:3, 4; 34:17)).

If you are trapped at this altar under a pile of fleshly bondages know it is not too late for repentance, reconciliation and restoration. Our flesh must be brought under subjection. If not, everyone connected to us pays a penalty.

Conclusion: Relationship of rebellion.

1. Imbalance between spiritual and carnal man

2. Lack of body discipline.

3RD ALTAR DECLARATION OF FAITH

PURPOSE: CIRCUMCISION OF HEART

GILGAL - ROLLING OFF AND AWAY

JOSHUA 5:2-9 CIRCUMCISION RENEWED, 5:10-11 PASSOVER, 5:12 MANNA CEASED

The reproach is gone and redemption is made possible.

Joshua erects a tombstone. Israel perceived all uncircumcised males as unclean and in a state of gross impurity. Circumcising the children of Israel, at this place, signified the reproach of Israel was rolled away. Lay the stone: To lay the stones had three implications: First, it was to set up tombstones for the previous generation that died in the wilderness because of disobedience.

Second, it was a sign the reproach was rolled off Israel. Third, it was to be a sign for all future generations to know they have the right to be free. They now have the right to enter into the fulfillment of the promise given by God. This is a deeper consecration, which releases the anointing, and God's glorious wonders.

Altar of

Exposure-illuminates the things that hold you hostage.

Praise-for what He has gloriously performed.

Anointing-empowers you to perform service.

This altar God defines:

1. Purification of heart and spirit.
2. Who He is: only by seeing God properly can a person see himself properly.

When you spend time in God's presence, you learn by experience, who He is and how great He is. This knowledge and wisdom forms a foundation and standard that influences your daily decisions. It will expose and build God's true character inwardly. This altar brings you <u>out of reproach</u> and <u>into redemption</u> (Duet 6: 23, Jos. 5:9).

God had performed a notable miracle for Israel. He had dried up the Jordan River in the time of its flooded state. This let all Israel's enemies know that God was with them; as a result, they became very afraid of them and their God. Because of the mighty feat, Israel let praise have its perfect work in their hearts toward a wonderful and awesome God.

Here the spiritual man is delivered from all its enemies. The inner man is called into covenant with God. Covenant always requires the shedding of blood. Therefore, circumcision was an outward sign that brought about a deeper consecration and relationship (covenant) with God. This deeper lifestyle deals with three elements: righteousness, purity and obedience in the heart. When the heart is clean and clear it communes with God in an atmosphere of love, peace and joy. The spirit is grateful for this pureness and praises God regardless of its outer surroundings.

Test: To purify the heart and spirit of man, so fear and doubt is not an option.

Trial: To make yourself an available vessel so God may do mighty and glorious wonders through and for you (Jos. 4:21-25).

CHANGE YOUR POSITION
Change My Attitude

You are Holy Ghost Filled

The Holy Ghost is here to lead and guide us in all truth. It is the Spirit that matures us into these truths (John 16:13). The Holy Ghost (Spirit) searches all things (I Cor. 2:10). He knows the deepest secrets buried within the heart. He knew the heart and mind of Judas, the betrayer of Jesus (John 13:21-27). Jeremiah 23:23-24 states, "Am I a God at hand, saith the Lord, and not a God afar off? Can any hide himself in secret places that I shall not see him? saith the Lord. Do not I fill heaven and earth? saith the Lord." David states there is no place to go where God is not (Psalm 139).

The mind, heart and body are purified and the Holy Ghost can fill the entire vessel. The Holy Spirit will not dwell in an unclean (filthy) temple. The triune spirit man is now in covenant with the triune God; therefore it praises God for His greatness (Ps. 48:1; 95:3-5).

Our text Joshua 5:2-9, deals both Old and New Testament Circumcision:

A. Old sign - Circumcision of Flesh (Gen. 17:10-14)

Old Testament Circumcision became the external token of the covenant between God and His people. It was a sign of initiation to show you belong to this group. Circumcision: (Heb. mula; Gk. peritome, a cutting around). The ceremony of circumcision consists in cutting away the foreskin, i.e., the hood or fold of skin covering the head of the male organ. It was done with a sharp knife, but in Josh. 5:2, a flint knife was used. It occurs on the eighth day after birth; when a new life cycle began, the child entered into covenant with God.

Of all the Covenants between God and man, the one most highly honored by the Jews, was that made with Abraham. Why do you suppose this is true? It is because this Covenant required primarily implicit faith and belief in Gods Word? After God had made a covenant with Abraham He commanded a specific ritual:

"He that is born in thy house, and he that is bought with thy money, must need be circumcised; and my covenant shall be in your flesh for an everlasting covenant" (Gen. 17:13). Circumcision was a visible mark in the male's reproductive organ that a Jewish male had been separated unto God. As a Jewish citizen, he could partake of the Passover. Unless this ceremony was performed, males could not become part of the Covenant community. Without circumcision, it was impossible to enjoy Abraham's blessings. Every one not circumcised was to be "cut off from his people" as having "broken My covenant" (Gen. 17:6-14; Ex. 12:43-49).

We must look for the significance of this rite in the fact that the corruption of sin usually manifests itself with peculiar energy in the sexual life, and that sanctification of the life was symbolized by the purifying of the organ by which life is reproduced. However, as spiritual purity was demanded of the chosen people of God, circumcision became its outward sign of covenant. It secured to the one subjected to it all the rights of the covenant, participation in all its material and spiritual benefits; while on the other hand, he was bound to fulfill all the covenant obligations. Figuratively circumcision was used a s a symbol of heart purity (Duet. 10:16; 30:6; Lev. 26:41; Jer. 4:4, 9:25-26; Ezek. 44:7). It is also figurative of a readiness to hear and obey (Jer. 6:10).

During the wilderness journey, they failed to circumcise the males. This negligence is most satisfactorily explained as follows: The nation while bearing the punishment of disobedience in its wanderings was regarded as under temporary rejection by God and therefore prohibited from using the sign of the covenant.

As the Lord promised His assistance on condition that the law given by Moses was faithfully observed, it became the duty of Joshua upon entering Canaan, to perform the rite of circumcision upon the generation that had been born in the wilderness. This was done immediately upon crossing the Jordan, at or near Gilgal. (Josh. 5:2-8). This act brought God's people back in alignment with Him.

Circumcision is practiced by today's society because of physical or health advantages. The removal of the foreskin prevents diseases and helps maintain cleanliness. It has no spiritual value for the medical society.

B. New sign - Circumcision of the Heart (Rom. 2:28-29; Col. 2:11-12)

New Testament Circumcision: On the Day of Pentecost, the sign that one had entered into Covenant was replaced with a new identification mark. Circumcision of heart is to cut away the hidden sin (iniquity) of the heart. While the Israelites were circumcised in the flesh, spiritual Israelites are circumcised in the heart (New Testament Christians). **"In whom also ye are circumcised with the circumcision made without hands, in putting off the body of the sins of the flesh by the circumcision of Christ; <u>Buried with him in baptism</u>, wherein also ye are <u>risen with him</u> through the faith of the operation of God, who hath raised him from the dead"** (Col. 2:11-12).

"For he is not a Jew, which is one outwardly; neither is that circumcision, which is outward in the flesh; But he is a Jew, which is one inwardly; and <u>circumcision is that of the heart</u>, in the spirit,.." (Rom. 2:28-29)

Christians are said to be circumcised in Christ (Col. 2:11). This circumcision is asserted to be "circumcision made without hands," that is a spiritual reality and not a physical rite. God desires to touch the very heart of man. The goal of this altar is to mold your heart with His compassion; transform your mind into right standing with God; and conform your will to His will. The Lord desires for the heart to conform itself into brokenness, righteousness and holiness, so that it will love, teach and touch a dying world with tenderness and compassion (Ps. 51:9-17).

David wrote Psalm 51 after Nathan told him he sinned and iniquity lay in his heart (II Samuel 11:1-12:15). Psalm 51 states: "Have mercy upon me, O God, according to Your lovingkindness; according to the multitude of Your tender mercies blot out my transgressions. Wash me thoroughly from my iniquity, and cleanse me from my sin. For I acknowledge my transgressions, and my sin is always before me. Against You, You only, have I sinned, and done this evil in Your sight—That you may be found just when You speak, and blameless when You judge. Behold, I was brought forth in iniquity, and in sin my mother conceived me. Behold, You desire truth in the inward parts, and in the hidden part You will make me to know wisdom. Purge me with hyssop, and I shall be clean; Wash me, and I shall be whiter than snow. Make me hear joy and gladness, that the bones You have broken may rejoice. Hide Your face from my sins, and blot out all my iniquities. Create in me a clean heart, O God, and renew a steadfast spirit within me. Do not cast away me from Your presence, and do not take Your Holy Spirit from me. Restore to me the joy of Your salvation, and uphold me by Your generous Spirit. Then I will teach transgressors Your ways, and sinners shall be converted to You. Deliver me from the guilt of blood-shed, O God, the God of my salvation, and my tongue shall sing aloud of Your righteousness. O Lord, open my lips, and my mouth shall show forth Your praise. For You do not desire sacrifice, or else I would give it; You do not delight in burnt offering. The sacrifices of God are a broken spirit, a broken and a contrite heart—these, O God, You will not despise. Do good in Your good pleasure to Zion; build the walls of Jerusalem. Then You shall be pleased with the sacrifices of righteous-ness, with burnt offering and whole burnt offering; then they shall offer bulls on Your altar."

To sin or error is human, but to persist in sin is foolish and devilish. Here, David is stating, sin is detrimental therefore, <u>we can't afford to continue in this hidden sin (iniquity) of the heart</u>. Iniquity is persistent wrongdoing and is a manifestation of evil. When iniquity is in the heart, it breaks fellowship between God and mankind. We must ask forgiveness so He may remove sin and restore this broken fellowship. We must ask Him to "Create in me a clean (pure) heart." A heart that earnestly desire to know and serve Jesus Christ in purity and righteousness. We are asking for a heart that is cleaned and purified of all wrongdoing and evil. In order to get a clean heart we must humble ourselves, acknowledge our wrong and forsake sin (I Kings 21:27-29; Isa. 1:16, 17; Joel 2:12, 13; Ps. 15, 24:3-5). When we repent and acknowledge our sins, God changes our heart; so we may walk blamelessly in His statues. In addition, He is willing to conform completely to His Word regardless to the cost. Therefore, when we go to God we ask Him to cut the pain and guilt out our heart.

Nicodemus (a Pharisee, a scholar, member of the Sanhedrin court and a ruler over the Jews) came to Jesus by night. He came at night because he feared being seen with Jesus could jeopardize his position. Nicodemus was a powerful man, but after seeing Jesus he realized something was missing inwardly. So he asked Him, how can a man be born again? Can he enter into his mother's womb and be born again? Jesus told him he had to be born of water and of the Spirit to enter the kingdom of God. He had to be transformed in his heart and abandon some of his traditions and values (John 3:1-10).

Next, we ask Him to "Renew a right spirit" (remove unrighteousness). It is with our spirit we communicate with God. Thus, our "inward parts desire to know truth and wisdom" of God first, then His Word. We seek to have a spirit free from impurities and contaminates. A spirit untainted by any of the ills of the Devil. When we are afflicted, we must not let it penetrate the heart with unrighteous thoughts and deeds. If we do, the heart becomes wounded and bitter. Spiritual wounds are wounds to the heart, not the mind. When the heart is sick, the whole body is sick. Out of the heart flow the issues of life and death. Such wounds will affect the way a person thinks and feels, but wounds to the spirit are not to the soul.

Forgiveness is the answer to the heart and spirit healing. It will return the spirit to right standing (righteousness) with God. It opens the heart, and releases blessings and hope. Forgiveness demands us to let go of inner pain. Inner pain is a powerful force. It can drive an otherwise normal person to extreme behavior, often yielding in very tragic results. Forgiveness goes beyond altar two and addresses the underlying issues of why we smoke, drink, lie, fornicate, etc. The circumstance creates pain, which causes anger, resentment, bitterness and hatred. This altar is after the hidden feelings of abandonment isolation, and low self-esteem. None of these things belong to you, they are lies infiltrated to your inner man, by the Devil. Unforgiveness is a hindrance to our prayers. It closes heaven's doors to us, thus leaving our prayers unanswered. In this state of unforgivesness, fellowship is broken and we remain closed, we blame and stay stuck in despair. Isa 1:15 NKJVstates, "When you spread out your hands, I will hide My eyes from you; Even though you make many prayers, I will not hear. Your hands are full of blood."

The Lord's Prayer tells us to forgive those who trespass against us; by the same measure that we forgive in (Matt. 6:9-15). Forgiveness is an act of obedience to God and His Word (Matt. 6:14; Luke 17:3-4; Eph. 4:32; Col. 3:13). When you do this, you permit God to work in you (Gen. 50:20; Duet. 32:4; Rom. 8:28-29, 38-39). This forgiveness places you in a state of righteousness so the heart is purified of all evil. You are in a higher state of consciousness to perform only what is good, pure and holy. The heart is undefiled and conditioned to respond with a right attitude, action, reaction and response no matter what the intent. Peace has permeated your heart and all fears and doubts are removed. You know that things will work out for your good, despite how they appear. This altar requires change in your prayer life. This preparation demands you to raise above all earthly obstacles and bondages. It is here purification declares a heart and spirit of love, joy, peace and freedom. The spirit is so loving, joyous, and peaceful and free it can only release obedience and praise toward an awesome and loving God. You are now empowered to receive the blessings and promises of God.

The New Testament is preparing for the Lord to have complete ownership of your body spirit and soul by permitting the Holy Spirit to rule. Your mind, body and heart are in harmony with God and His Word. The Holy Spirit rises to a higher and more meaningful level within you. All heart desires are transformed yielded and conformed to the will of God. We are given God's wisdom and His grace to become righteous and we overcome our evil tendencies or habits. We become mature in the spirit.

When evil knocks, righteousness withstands it and refuses to abuse or violate mercy and grace. We are given the power to reject sin and grace to clothe ourselves with God's righteousness (Rom 5:20, 6:1-5). "Therefore, put on God's complete armor, that you may be able to resist and stand your ground in the evil day [of danger], and, having done all, [the crisis demands], to stand [firmly in your place]. Stand therefore [hold your ground], having tightened the belt of truth around your loins and having put on the breastplate of (righteousness) integrity and of moral rectitude and right standing with God. And having shod your feet in the preparation [to face the enemy with the firm-footed stability, the promptness, and the readiness produced by the good news] of the Gospel of peace. [Isa. 52:7.] Lift up over all the [covering] shield of "saving faith, upon which you can quench all the flaming missiles of the wicked [one]. And take the helmet of salvation and the sword that the Spirit wields, which is the Word of God. Pray at all times (on every occasion, in every season) in the Spirit, with all [manner of] prayer and entreaty. To that end keep alert and watch with strong purpose and perseverance, interceding in behalf of all the saints (God's consecrated people). And [pray] also for me, that [freedom of] utterance may be given me, that I may open my mouth to proclaim boldly the mystery of the good news (the gospel)" (Eph. 6:13-19). Righteousness must be practiced to develop it into your lifestyle. Our relationship, our history, our lifestyle, our holy place of consecration and purity in Christ permits us to wear this robe of righteousness. God is calling all men unto righteousness (I Thess. 4:3). Without it no man shall see God (Heb. 12:14). This is a permanent place of authority and victory over the Devil (Ps. 1:1-6).

The Holy Spirit has come to lead and guide us on earth (Rom. 8:14). There are many Christians who never make it to this third altar therefore they will continue to lead a defeated lifestyle. They don't understand that Paul speaks clearly in Gal. 5:18, "But if you are led by the Spirit you are not under the law," you now are sons of God. This sonship entitles you to all benefits. The benefit is for you to live under grace not the law. For the law couldn't be kept by humanity anyway. Grace says, I submit my will to the Holy Spirit, therefore, I will not have to struggle anymore for He will guide and lead me into righteous living. When we rely on the Holy Spirit He knows the pathway we need to take for the fulfillment and productivity in Christ. Why don't you invite Him in today?

We must ask for a clean heart and a renewed spirit because the Holy Ghost will not dwell in an unclean spirit. This circumcision of the heart makes way for a purified and holy heart, which now is ready for Him (Holy Spirit) to enter with all truths. He enters with the truth of Jesus, the Word and Himself. This is the way we check for authenticity and righteousness; the harmony of all three should bear witness with each other. Are they all saying the same thing? If so truth abounds (I John 5:6). The essence and value of this altar is to be baptized in the Holy Spirit. This is a gift (Luke 11:13) received through Jesus redemptive work on the cross and grace through faith (Acts 1:52, 2:38-39). The evidence of being spirit filled or baptized in the Holy Spirit is speaking is tongues (Acts 2:2-4, 10:44-46, 19:6, 8:14-17). The miracles that Jesus performed were because God, the Father lived inside Him. He has given us the same power to do even greater works than He has done (John 14:12). If we make ourselves available to His Holy Spirit, we can achieve mighty and wondrous things. The compassion and power of God will flow out of your heart. We shall lay hands on the sick, cast out demons, raise the dead and set the captive free, etc. (Mark 16:17). The Holy Ghost comes to empower you for service! This altar empowers you to shift the environment. We see and feel the shift in the spiritual realm first, and then see it manifested in the natural second. Therefore, when we get to the last altar, the walls must come down.

2. Next, our text deals with the Passover at this altar. The Passover is celebrated in remembrance of their deliverance from Egypt. This was a reminder that God spared their firstborn (Ex. 12:27). The prophetic significance is depicting Christ as our Passover for this day (John 1:29, 19:36; I Cor. 5:7; I Pet. 1:18-19). The Passover is the

foundation for the Lord's Supper (Matt. 26:17-30; Mark 14:12-25; Luke 22:1-20). Unleavened bread was used as a sign to commemorate the hardships of Israel's flight from Egypt (Ex. 12:39). It was to symbolize consecration and devotion to God, two very key components of this altar. The unleavened bread also was a type of Christ (John 6:30-59; I Cor. 11:24); and a type of the true church (I Cor. 5:7-8). We also see the Passover as foreshadowing the marriage supper of the Lamb (Matt. 26:29; Mark 14:25; Luke 22:16-18). The key elements for us today are: to remember how, why and from what God has delivered us; because of our love for Him, we remain devoted and consecrated to Him.

3. Finally, manna ceased; God is preparing them to enter into a new land. Everything had changed. Whenever you proceed to another level, their must be a transformation. What sustained you at this place is not sufficient for where he is leading you. God wanted to reveal Himself in a new and different way. The biggest challenge is to seek Him in a new, unfamiliar and uncomfortable way. Israel no longer needed God to perform miracles to feed them. The manna was a reminder that God would

keep His Promise to them. He would provide for them until they reached the Promise Land. Therefore, six days weekly for forty years, their provisions fell from the sky in the form of manna. God kept His promises they entered the new land; then the manna ceased. It no longer fell from the heavens, but now provisions came from the ground. God was instituting a new thing in this new land. God sent them into the land when it was very productive and fertile, so they felt no lack or shortage. Their provision now came from the inherited ground, therefore He wanted them to feed themselves, which was a metaphor that they desired to seek Him because they loved Him and not out of duty or the need for provision (Matt 6:33).

God requires excellence in our inward parts. At this altar, the flesh is dead to sin; it walks in the Spirit so it will not fulfill the works of the flesh. It recognizes when sin tries to raise its filthy head, therefore it resists.

We must remember at the altars God is in control of our lives. Our lives must be subject to change at any given moment. This change no longer sees things as they are but sees them the way God sees them. We refuse captivity and calls freedom into our earthly realm and the blessing is manifested.

Conclusion: Relationship of Righteousness, change of heart.

1. The heart is purged of evil.
2. The heart is filled with the Holy Spirit.
   a. Love and forgiveness rules.
3. The believer is now empowered for service.

3RD BAAL ALTAR
RENDER THE HEART EVIL

PURPOSE: TO MAKE THE
HEART BITTER

At this altar, the Devil chooses to control the heart by way of deception. At this point, the person has become accustomed to rebellion. They have acquired a taste and a consistency for repeating the same sin over and over again. Usually the penalty has not been seen yet, so why stop. It now becomes iniquity of the heart because it is hidden.

Altar of
Deception-the Devil makes it appears
there is no hope for redemption.
Complaint-you murmur and complain against
God and His Word.

Fear and Doubt-render you powerless to
accept and perform miracles.

This altar seeks
1. Control of the spirit.
2. Control of the heart.

Also James 1:22 states, "But be doers of the word, and not hearers only, deceiving your own self." In other words the hearer must obey and love truth (II Thess. 2:10), if not danger lies at his door. The danger that the believer must heed is the deception that enters the heart. Deception is the practice of deliberately making somebody believe things that are not true; an act; a trick or device intended to deceive or mislead somebody. The Devil is the father of lies and it is through deception that he tricks the believer and sways his heart from God. Deception is his primary tool to keep humanity under his control. Take away his seductive powers and you will see his true offer of hell. Rev. 12:9 AMP states, "And the huge dragon was cast down and out—that age old serpent, who is called the Devil and Satan, he who is the seducer (deceiver) of all humanity the world over..."

Below are two parables (short stories) which evoke thought, decision and action. In Matthew 13:14-15 NKJV, the people saw, heard and clearly understood the truth but they refused and rejected it. They continued in their path of unrighteousness until, step by step, there hearts grew exceedingly cold and bitter. They grew insensitive and were deceived by old religious traditions and forms of godliness, but denying the true repentance and power of God. Jesus stated these words, "*And in them the prophecy of Isaiah is fulfilled, which says: Hearing you will hear and shall not understand, and seeing you will see and not perceive; for the hearts of this people have grown dull. Their ears are hard of hearing, and their eyes have closed. Lest they should see with their eyes and hear with their ears, lest they should understand with their hearts and turn, so that I should heal them.*" In their stubborn hearts, they would not repent so they continue to reject and disobey the truth.

Further insight is given in Matthew 13:18-22 NKJV, "*Therefore hear the parable of the sower: When anyone hears the word of the kingdom, and does not understand it, then the wicked one comes and snatches it away what was sown in his heart. This is he who received seed by the wayside. But he who received the seed on stony places, this is he who hears the word and immediately receives it with joy; yet he has no root in himself, but endures only for a while. For when tribulation or per-secution arises because of the word, immediately he stumbles. Now he who received seed among the thorns is he who hears the word, and the cares of this world and the deceitfulness of riches choke the word, and he becomes unfruitful."* The devil is always trying to steal the Word of God out of the heart and mind. He knows it is the Word of God that cleanses and purifies our hearts. So he will make your hearing dull, your heart hardened, your eyes blinded and your understanding lack reason.

If we refuse to maintain our heart with the Word of God, we will continually walk in disobedience. When a person disobeys the Word of God clearly revealed, it is at that very moment a *veil goes over his heart,* and that veil distorts and obstructs his spiritual and physical view. When we first were saved and we sinned, we felt conviction. We felt as though a knife stabbed our heart although it was the Holy Spirit, which was calling for true repentance. Now if we truly repented, our hearts were cleaned and purified as we were restored. However, if we justify (make excuses), our behavior we did not truly repent, therefore two circumstances arise. First, we open ourselves to disobedience and willfully repeat the same sin (act of disobedience). Second, this veil covers our hearts (iniquity); therefore lessening the sense of conviction and replacing it with reasoning. We spiritually turn a death ear to the Holy Spirit, the Word of God and the principle of truth (morals). Therefore, the next time we feel this pain; it doesn't hurt as much because a veil has shrouded (burial cloth) it. We no longer feel a knife; we feel a pinch of discomfort. When we continue to justify our behavior and we willfully disobey, another veil blankets our hearts and muffles further callings of the truth. Therefore, if again we chose to sin, we now sense a mere tingle of conviction in our hearts. Again, if we justify, another death shroud veils our hearts. If we sin again, the veil is so thick there is no conviction at all, only justification.

The source of right or wrong is no longer drawn in the heart from the Word of God or by the Holy Spirit. At this point, the person walks boldly into whatever the father of lies (Satan) convey to them. God will still try to reach the man stuck in disobedience. His first, attempt is through conviction; but if he continues to disobey, it signifies the heart is veiled by deception. This man has lost touch with God's directives, so God sends a prophetic messenger, He sent Samuel to Saul. Finally, if sin is repeated God attempts to reach by judgment. "For if we *judge* ourselves, we should not be *judged*" (I Cor. 11:31 NKJV). The first part of this scripture is telling us if we examine ourselves thoroughly to remove iniquity from the heart, we won't be judged.

David committed adultery and was a murderer, but kept doing business as usual. He acted as though nothing happened. He continued as King in regular forms of worship. David's heart was far from God just as many Christians are today. They outwardly pretend to be godly but inwardly they are not walking with God. It took the Prophet Nathan for David to come to terms with his sinful heart (II Sam. 12). He needed to repent, confess his sin and turn away from sin. Revival can only come when truth is revealed (Prov. 28:13). Daniel told Nebuchadnezzar to break off thy sins (Dan. 4:27). Are you continuing in some form of sin in your life; break it off, stop it immediately?

Does God judge or punish His people when they refuse to hear prophetic warning? He is not an evil God; it is you who removed yourself from under His safety net with constant sin. God will not remain in the presence of sin; so when you distant yourself from Him and His Word, you give the Devil an open door to harm you. The answer usually comes in some sort of hardship, sickness or possible affliction. The Psalmist David declared, Before I was afflicted I went astray, But now I keep Your word... I know, O Lord, that Your judgments are right, And that in faithfulness You have afflicted me (Ps. 119:67, 75 NKJV). Saul refused to hear the Prophet Samuel and he moved himself away from God.

Pride is a form of dangerous deception. It was the downfall of Lucifer. *How you are fallen from heaven, O Lucifer, son of the morning! How you are cut down to the ground, You who weakened the nations! For you have said in your heart: I will ascend into heaven. I will exalt my throne above the stars of God; I will also sit on the mount of the congregation on the farthest sides of the north; I will ascend above the heights of the clouds, I will be like the Most High. Yet you shall be brought down to Sheol, to the lowest depths of the*

Pit (Isa. 14:12-15). Lucifer's heart was filled with pride and it corrupted his wisdom and beauty (Ez. 28:12-17). A prideful heart has caused many men and women to fall. Satan will use pride to tempt humanity to error. This error is sin, which draws the heart away from truth and fills it with a false imagination.

Another form of dangerous deception is self-righteousness. Self-righteousness is an enemy of God; it is excessive belief in your own virtue. The enemy permits this spirit to creep in with the deceptive vice that the believer is walking in true authority, but actually, he is operating in a form of spirituality without personal deliverance. The Devil does this by confronting the believer only with situations he can handle. This keeps him in a mindset of believing he is victorious when he is not even involved in warfare. In actuality, they are not confronting the enemy; therefore, he doesn't confront them with anything they can not handle. He never confronts them with things that would cause them to depend upon God. He also tries to keep the believer from other Christians who would challenge a higher level and dependency in God.

The second issues at this altar are the spirit of complaint. Complaint is a formal charge against someone that has caused a problem; a statement expressing discontent or unhappiness about a situation. Wherever you find deception and the need for justification, complaining will immediately follow. If you check all through the scriptures you will find the three (deception, justification, and complaint) in unison and cohesive order. When Satan deceived Adam and Eve, it was subtle but huge. He made Eve feel God was withholding something good from them. Therefore, the Devil attacked God's righteous character and His wisdom for mankind through deception and distortion. He got Eve to question God's goodness, generosity and integrity. She was beguiled into disobedience, but Adam went willfully (Gen. 3:1-7 NKJV). Eve justified eating from the fruit when she thought God was withholding the right to be as gods; knowing good and evil. Adam's justification was once Eve ate and she didn't die that it was okay for him to eat of the fruit. God imparted his word to Adam, but which part of the inner man did not become submitted to the truth and the Word of God. Satan slid through an unlocked door and twisted the truth. The

Devil is the father of deception and a master manipulator (John 8:44 NKJV), was at work in the garden. After he manipulated them into eating the fruit he became there evil lord. "Do you not know that to whom you present yourselves to obey, you are that one's slave whom you obey, whether sin leading to death, or of disobedience leading to unrighteousness?"

When God called Adam on the carpet, his first complaint was about Eve the woman You (God) gave me. He was implying God was the blame, since He gave her to him. Eve's complaint was the serpent (Gen. 3:10-14). The devil's deception leads to disobedience, disobedience leads to rebellion; rebellion leads to iniquity; and continued iniquity leads to apostasy.

Israel would not take responsibility for her action; she continued to conceal her evil and disobedient hearts. She blamed everyone and everything for her failure. Israel lodged so many complaints she wandered forty years because of it: she complained about God's, leader Moses, food, water and being in a strange land, etc.

Moses was a complainer (Ex. 3:13; 4:1, 10, 13; 5: 22; 6:12, 30; Num. 11:11, 21); and so was the people who followed him. As each complaint was lodged to Moses, he complained to God. The people placed Moses under so much pressure and despair that he requested to die (Num. 11:10-15). Although God provided Israel with miracles to meet all her needs, they continually showed distrust, dissatisfaction and a lack of appreciation. Israel's chief complaint was food and water (Ex. 15:24-26; 16:2-8; 17:3-7); three were about jealousy, (Num. 12:1-16; 16:1-35; 17:1-13); and two prompted fear, bitterness and cowardice, (Num. 14:2-38; 16:41-50).

Complaining is an enemy of praise. It will separate you from God and bring judgment into your life. God is slow to anger (Ps. 103:9, 145:8), but Israel's history shows that she repeatedly provoked God to anger. Israel had sunk very low in sin (idolatry) and moral depravity during the absence of Moses. He was so tired of Israel's disobedience and complaining. Four times God planned to destroyed her [the nation](Ex. 32:7-10; Num. 14:11; 16:20, 44) but Moses interceded on her behalf and she was spared (Ex. 32:30; 33:12; 34:8; Num. 14:13; 16:22). Although Israel was spared, she was not exempt from punishment for her rebellion (Ex. 32:20, 25, 33).

The last problem at this altar is fear and doubt, it will render you powerless. Fear and doubt are twins. The two are powerful tools used by the Devil to immobilize Christian actions.

Let's look at Saul's history. His life will reveal important lessons of obedience and disobedience to the believer. Here also you will see deception, justification and complaint by Israel. Samuel was the prophet in that day; he also held the office of a priest and a judge (I Sam. 7:9-15). He was growing old, and he appointed his sons judges over Israel, but the people saw their dishonesty and refused their leadership (I Sam. 8:4-5). Although Samuel served wholeheartedly he, wouldn't examine nor correct his children's wrongdoing. After this Israel desired a king, so they could be like the heathen nations. They thought a king would help them win their battles. They didn't realize they were losing because of disobedience. Samuel told them God was their king and they did not need an earthly king. He stated a king would oppress them, but Israel rejected him and demanded a king. So God gave them their own selfish (*lusty*) desires and granted a king (I Sam. 8: 22).

In Israel, we see disobedience (Baal altar 1), lust (Baal altar 2) and now deception (Baal altar 3). You might ask where does the deception lies? They heard the Word of the Lord, but would not do (obey) it, so they deceived themselves. Israel used Samuel's dishonest sons as an excuse to justify her desire for a king. Her complaint she lodged was God was withholding something good from her. She desired to be as the heathen nations who appeared to do well. She thought an earthly king could solve her problems. She was foolish to think an earthly king could do more than a heavenly Father could. It is only God who can rise up and pull down nations and strongholds of the heart.

Saul was the first king to be appointed over Israel. Each king was anointed and given a prophet. The Prophet Samuel was assigned to King Saul. Saul had a salvation experience and was given a new heart (I Sam. 10:9). God granted Saul to be gifted inward (spiritually) and outward (naturally). He also provided victory to defeat the Ammonites, which gave the people great confidence and hope in him as king (I Sam. 10:1-12). Saul was destined to be great until he became impatient. Samuel told Saul to go to Gilgal and wait seven days and he would come and offer sacrifice to the Lord. Saul became impatient and chose not to wait, so he violated the priestly office by offering a sacrifice. Samuel did come as he stated but the damage was already done. It was too late for Saul; he disobeyed and was rejected by God as king, due to his self-will and impatience (I Sam. 13:1-15).

In I Samuel chapter 15, we see Saul doing his own thing again. God wants all or nothing. He prefers you to be hot or cold. He partially carried out God's command. He was told to destroy the Amalekites and everything they had. God commanded Saul to kill the king, every man and woman, infant and nursing child, ox and sheep, camel and donkey. Did Saul do it? No! His own selfish greed and rebellious spirit chose to disobey the specific word given to him by the prophet. He spared Agag, the king of the Amalekites, and took for himself the best of their livestock.

When Samuel confronted Saul about his disobedience, first he said he obeyed; then, he tried to justify by offering a lame excuse that he was going to sacrifice the livestock unto the Lord. In I Samuel 15:22 NKJV, it states these words: Has the Lord as great delight in burnt offerings and sacrifices, as in obeying the voice of the Lord? Behold, to obey is better than sacrifice, and to heed than the fat of rams. For rebellion is as the sin of witchcraft, and stubbornness is as iniquity and idolatry.

Saul's complaint was lodged against Israel, he tried to blame her for his action of disobedience. I Samuel 15:24 records: Then Saul said to Samuel, I have sinned; for I have transgressed the commandment of the Lord and your words; for I feared the people and obeyed their voice. Because you have rejected the word of the Lord, He also has rejected you from being king. Samuel called sin what it is, a blatant disregard and disrespect for God and His Word.

Although Saul pleaded and begged for forgiveness, he was still rejected. It is only a matter of time before a person's heart reveals its true nature: soft and obedient towards the Lord or hard and self-serving towards themselves. Samuel and God knew his disobedient heart and rebellious spirit, and this numbered his days as king and ended his promising reign. Samuel carried out the Lord's word and destroyed King Agag (I Samuel 15:1-36). Saul's story will continue at the next altar.

The spirits at work at this altar are spirit of infirmity, dumb and deaf spirit, spirit of bondage, and spirit of fear.

Conclusion: Relationship of Deception
1. The heart is deceived.
2. It justifies continual wrongdoing.

4ᵀᴴ ALTAR REVELATION OF FAITH

PURPOSE: MANIFESTATION OF THE GLORY OF GOD

JERICHO-CITY of the MOON

THE WALLS CAME DOWN JOSHUA 6:1-21

God sends the answer to your request: This is the Devils last stand and it doesn't disturb you at all. The Devil states you are defeated. God has implanted a personal promise and scripture inside you. You are so tuned into God and his Word that when the enemy comes in like flood, God will raise up a standard against him (Isa. 59:19). It is here, a man recognizes it is all or nothing. Man is so confident in God, he is willing to stand up against the wiles of the devil and die for Christ. After you have done all to stand, you will stand unshaken and unmovable (Eph. 6: 11-17). He has tasted of God's glory and it doesn't compare to the suffering of this world. He is so caught up in the presence of God; his desire is to remain in His presence forever (II Cor. 5:6-9).

There are four things that take place at this altar: 1) Joshua hearkens (yields) unto the Lord; 2) he obeys His command; 3) he aligns himself with the will of God; 4) the glory of God is revealed.

Altar of

Worship: You are consumed by the presence of God.

Manifestation: God has given you a promise from His Word;

a) God shows up mightily on your behalf,

b) and perform the miracle needed.

Glory of God: He shows up mightily and declares He is the True and Living God.

This altar defines:

1. Who God is!

2. Declares His Power and Deity!

At this altar, the body, the heart and the soul have been purified and are in complete accordance of righteousness (right standing with God). All outward desires have ceased and everything is working in the spirit. There are no words only sounds of glory. There is a consuming fire, which burns up everything that is not in its highest form of love, adoration and worship for God. Man becomes the sweet, innocent, pure, and holy fragrance of worship that is pleasing in God's sight.

The heart purification and circumcision brings you to complete submission and obedience to God's plan and purpose. Here every member of your being permeates oneness: mind, body, heart and soul. You have gone beyond the veil. The spiritual man enters the holy of holies. You are now in the divine presence of the true and living almighty God. There is nothing between you and God, no separation. Your soul is anchored: your faith arises to know only victory in your heart, and your spirit waits for the physical manifestation.

Test: To unify man's heart, body, mind and soul into the highest relationship with God.

Trial: To know God can do anything, but fail. He will use you to perform miracles.

CHANGE YOUR CIRMCUMSTANCES
Change My Altitude

You are Fired Baptized

Here you encounter the consuming fire of the Almighty God. It is here, at this altar, your total being is purified by fire. When we permit ourselves to go willing into the fire, we permit God to have His perfect way and will in us. This fire removes every impurity that hinders the baptized believer from becoming a valuable instrument in the Master's hand. Your faith is tried and proven; thus, making you authentic. This fire is so intense that it fills the mind, body and heart with intense feelings of passion for only God. Your desires are now whatever He desires. Every part of you is in total harmony and balance with the triune God. Nothing without can distract the whole being within. You now walk in excellence without any fear, turmoil or boundaries equipped to do God's will.

Relationship of Glory: It is at this altar you worship the headship of the trinity (God). Your worship is filled with honor, admiration, praise, thanksgiving, awesome splendor, exaltation and majesty towards a loving God. You now abide under the shadow of the true and living almighty God. Being in his presence is your heart's desire. You lay before him pure and holy, for you have built your relationship from each altar: altar one, Relationship of Fellowship; altar two, Relationship of Righteousness; altar three, Relationship of Holiness; altar four, Relationship of Glory; so God's desire is to bless and show you to all the world. God has called you for a specific task and it burns deep within.

When we examine the highlights and significance of each altar, we will find the following: At the first altar we saw a rock (representation of Jesus Christ) upon which Jacob laid his head; the second altar Jesus crushed the rocks and turned them into stones and Israel walked on them; the third altar there is a death and burial; they pick the stones up and carry them to a grave site. They became a tombstone and a memorial place was erected. Therefore, we are now at the last altar; and it is here we see a wall. From where did the wall come? Remember, I told you it is the Devil's last stance, so he throws everything he can at you. He creates an obstacle to distract your mind and vision from the victories you won. The Devil tries to render your vision fearful, doubtful, hopeless and finally helpless. He hopes the pressure and shock of another problem will derail, destroy or kill you. For this, is the altar where all circumstances are changed forever concerning this matter? The thing that has kept you and your family in bondage is all over; it is finished, done, never to raise its head again. Finally, the promised victory has come if you don't faint or get weary (Gal. 6:9). He who has begun a good work in you is able to complete it (Phil. 1:6). Quitting is not an option.

Grace is a key element at this altar; it is full of power, favor, love and kindness. It enables you to become stronger in your faith and introduces a deeper intimacy with Him. Grace is God granting supernatural strength to uphold you while you're in the midst of pain that He will not change. This grace ignites the determination in you to keep aiming towards God's goal. It states God is in control and something good will come out of this situation. This grace is sustaining faith that will bring you through. Grace enabled Stephen to stand, while being stoned, until heaven's door opened. It held Jesus to the cross, until he became a victor. Grace enabled Paul to keep the faith although he suffered much hardship (II Corinthians 11:23-28). He also was imprisoned, but he wrote much of the New Testament in prison. So good can come out a difficult situation. Since you desire and seek [perceptible] proof of the Christ Who speaks in and through me. [For He] is not weak and feeble in dealing with you, but is mighty power within you; For though He was crucified in weakness, yet He goes on living by the power of God. And though we too are weak in Him [as He was humanly weak], yet in dealing with you [we shall show ourselves] alive and strong in [fellowship with] Him by the power of God. Examine and test and evaluate your own selves to see whether you are holding to your faith and showing the proper fruits of it. Test and prove yourselves [not Christ]. Do you not yourselves realize and know [thoroughly by an ever-increasing experience] that Jesus Christ is in you—unless you are [counterfeits] disapproved on trial and rejected? But I hope you will recognize and know that we are not disapproved on trial and rejected. But I pray to God that you may do nothing wrong, not in order that we [our teaching] may appear to be approved, but that you may continue doing right, [though] we may seem to have failed and be unapproved. For we can do nothing against the Truth [not serve any party or personal interest], but only for the Truth [which is the Gospel]. For we are glad when we are weak (unapproved) and you are really strong. And this we also pray for: your all-round strengthening and perfecting of soul. v. 11...Be strengthened (perfected, completed, made what you ought to be); be encouraged and consoled and comforted; v. 14...The grace (favor and spiritual blessing) of the Lord Jesus Christ and the love of God and the presence and fellowship (the communion and sharing together, and participation) in the Holy Spirit be with you all (II Cor. 13:3-9, 11, 14 AMP).

In our text, Joshua is confronted with the walls of Jericho. It is human understanding and reasoning which goes out the window. In the natural realm you are inadequate but in the spiritual realm you are a giant. Here, at altar four, he is confronting the test and trial of his faith. Let us see what is recorded in the book of Joshua concerning him and these altars. This last altar is a summary of all four altars:

First, he was given a name; Joshua means, "Jehovah is salvation". You also will be given a name and told to "leave and cleave" when you complete the first altar. You are delivered from self.

Second, he is called, *"Moses my servant is dead: now therefore arise," (1:2).* This is the official call of Joshua by the Lord. This call has a precise law of timing. Although Moses called (appointed) him in Deut. 31:7-8, and he was sanctioned and ordained in Deut. 34:9, he had to wait on the Lord. Each man is called to salvation, obedience and faithfulness. You will be asked to change your plan and adjust to the plan of God after completing this second altar. It is, at this altar, that you are delivered from people. Joshua never had a problem with God, himself or the enemy; the problem lay within the people.

Third, he was commissioned, *"...go over this bank of Jordan, thou, and all this people, unto the land which I do give to them, even to the children of Israel" (1:2).* You will be asked to change your position and do the service (task) at hand at this third altar. The first task (personal) is to go home and save your household and extended family; next (corporate) you're neighbors and friends; and finally the world (Acts 1:8). It is your duty to disciple others. This is a huge task in itself. Secondly, you will be asked to do a special specific task (individual). This task is what you were created to do.

Fourth, he was given a promise, a word and a visitation, *"Every place that the sole of your foot shall tread upon, that have I given unto you, as I said unto Moses. From the wilderness and this Lebanon even unto the great river, the river Euphrates, all the land of the Hittites, and unto the great sea toward the going down of the sun, shall be your coast" (1:3-4).* You too will be given a promise: 1) individual, and 2) corporate.

This promise is a declaration, a decree, a vow of assurance that this pledge will be done by God. Furthermore it has granted you spiritual insight and foreknowledge in the spiritual realm. The total essence of this insight is to encourage you to hold on until the actual promise is manifested into the natural realm. To be a victor, you must wait for the results. Though the vision tarries, wait on it (Hab. 2:3).

And he was given a word to sustain his faith, *"There shall not any man be able to stand before thee all the days of thy life: as I was with Moses, so I will be with thee: I will not fail thee, nor forsake thee" (1:5).* The Lord foresees the great attack at this altar so he gives Joshua further word and exhortation to sustain him during this test and trial, *"<u>be strong and of good courage</u>: for unto this people shalt thou divide for an inheritance the land, which I sware unto their fathers to give them. <u>Only be thou strong and very courageous</u>, that thou mayest observe to do according to all the law, which Moses my servant commanded thee: turn not from it to the right hand or to the left, that thou mayest prosper whithersoever thou goest. This book of the law shall not depart out of thy mouth; but thou shalt meditate therein day and night, that thou mayest observe to do according to all that is written therein: for then thou shalt make thy way prosperous, and then thou shalt have good success. Have not I commanded thee? <u>Be strong and of good courage; be not afraid, neither be thou dismayed; for the Lord thy God is with thee whithersoever thou goest"</u> (1:6-9).* Joshua is told to meditate day and night in this word. It is to be incorporated in the inner mind, body and spirit. You too will receive a word from God. This word will carry you through if you implant it deeply into your heart where no one can steal it. This was not the only time he heard this word. He heard these words, "Be of good courage" in Numbers 13:20 when he was sent out to spy out the land, and Deuteronomy 31:5-8 when he was counseled by Moses. These words were repeated to build spiritual strength (courage) and confidence in the inner man; thus, equipping the outer man to stand during the test.

He also received a visitation, *"And it came to pass, when Joshua was by Jericho, that he lifted up his eyes and looked, and behold, there stood a man over against him with a sword drawn in his hand and Joshua went unto him, and said unto him, Art thou for us, or for our adversaries? And he said, Nay but as captain of the host of the Lord am I now come. And Joshua fell on his face to the earth, and did worship, and said unto him, What saith my lord unto his servant? And the captain of the LORD'S host said unto Joshua, Loose thy shoe from off thy foot; for the place whereon thou standest is holy. And Joshua did so" (5:13-15).* Finally, you will have some type of visitation by God. This visitation will sanction the promise, encapsulate the word in your heart, mind and spirit to believe: *I can do all things through Christ that strengthens me (Phil. 4:13); I am more than a conquer (Rom. 8:37); and this too shall come to pass.* I can make it and victory belongs too me, it is truly mine. At this final altar, your circumstance is changed and the spiritual and physical manifestation of victory is evident. The old thing is going down but the new thing is coming up. The abstract becomes concrete, and the intangible becomes tangible. The promise, the word and the visitation is yours for life.

So let's deal with our text in reference to each altar:

First, they had to leave and cleave; they left Acacia Grove and went to the edge of Jordan … *you have not passed this way before (3:1-4).* This word is significant because it informs us that we were in a place we had never been before. This was a new territory, a new dimension, a new realm that calls for a change of mind. Don't expect the old or former things in this new place. Many will think this new territory is a hard place, but it is not. It is just different from the ordinary. Don't expect to worship God in the same way. A new relationship, territory and realm are established.

Second, it deals with sanctification at Jordan; *And Joshua said unto the people, "Sanctify yourselves, for tomorrow the Lord will do wonders among you" (3:5).* Again, cleanse yourself from physical (fleshly) unrighteousness. Once again, they are confronted with waters; instead of the Red Sea, it is the Jordan River. Water is always an element found in cleansing. These are the obstacles and events that confront them. In the:

Past, they were fleeing from the enemy.

Present, they are canceling the enemy within.

Future, they were chasing the enemy and overtaking them.

Don't expect God to bless your mess. He does not sanction filth, so <u>wash yourself, make yourself clean</u>, for He is a holy God.

Third, they dealt with circumcision and a memorial which led to a deeper consecration (setting apart); "And these stones shall be a memorial to the children of Israel forever (4:4-24 NKJV) emphasis on, *v. 20 And those twelve stones which they took from the Jordan, Joshua set up in Gilgal."* They were a reminder of God's power when He held back the waters of Jordan, and his faithfulness in bringing them <u>out</u> and <u>into</u> the land. Joshua was obedient to God and circumcised all the males born in the wilderness; the miracle was the men were healing from circumcision and could not fight, so God divinely protected Israel. The enemy was scared to attack them. They observed the Passover. The manna ceased falling for forty years six times a week. For the new land would produce food for them (5:1-12). Scripture confirms they are at the third altar. It is at this altar all forms of evil are cut out the heart and it is filled with love, joy and peace.

Joshua was encouraged by the prior miracles shown to him. He was not disturbed by the walls of Jericho. He knew if God did that, he would most certainly do this, if they obey the command of the Lord. *"Now faith is the substance of things hoped for, the evidence of things not seen (Hebrews 11:1).* Today we believe in God to bring forth tangible matter from what we want or expect to be true. The message bible records the same passage as: *The fundamental fact of existence is that this trust in God, this faith, is the firm foundation under everything that makes life worth living. It's our handle on what we can't see*. Last, they fought the battle and the glory of the Lord showed up at this fourth altar, Jericho.

This altar deals with three active elements of faith: seeing, hearing and shouting.

1. Seeing, And the Lord said to Joshua "*See!* I have given Jericho into your hand, its king, and the mighty men of valor;" this seeing is based on invisible truths revealed by the Word of God. The physical senses are connected to the physical world, therefore you must believe in the spiritual realm that God will provide and hold to his Word.

2. Hearing, when they make a long blast with the ram's horn, and when you *hear* the sound of the trumpet; the sound has a specific keen sound in the spiritual realm to heighten your beliefs in the unknown. Only faith can make the things of God a reality before you can receive them.

3. Shouting that all the people shall *shout with a great shout;* then the wall of the city will fall down flat. And the people shall go up every man straight before him"

(6:1-5 NKJV). Although this was a natural presentation, it was a spiritual seeing, hearing, and shouting that
provided faith to trust God for victory by such meager
means.

When we examine these verses closely, we will find
that Joshua was groomed to see victory in God through
all his prior adventures. He saw ten plagues pronounced
upon the Egyptians and not one harmed his people. He
saw God bring them out Egypt with a mighty hand and
part the Red Sea for them to cross over to the other side.
He saw Pharaoh and his army destroyed when they pur-
sued. When Joshua was sent to spy out the land, he saw
they could take the land. God is calling him to see per-
fection. He wants him to see in the spirit and not in the
fleshly realm.

Next sound has two different meaning and purposes
here in this scripture. First silence has a sound of submission and obedience. They were submitting to God's
authority and plan. Although marching around the walls
sound crazy, they chose to give up their judgment and
obey God. Obedience follows instructions and pays
special attention to details. One act of obedience can
ignite the world. Second, the quietness permitted them

to hear the sound of the Holy Spirit making intercession on their behalf.

Finally, they shouted. This shout was more than praise, for it brings you in the presence of God. This shout was on a higher frequency of worship. It ushers you into the chambers of God's rest, full of obedience and dependency upon Him. It is worship that loosens the hands of God and releases the answer.

This altar's goal is to test your endurance of faith in God. Every Christian will at some point reach a cross-road of faith, when he or she has to take a stand, even at the risk of personal loss. All Christians will face times of testing. They will have to <u>choose</u> rather they will stand for Christ or bow to Baal. It is during these times you must have confidence, courage and conviction in God to resist the Devil's evil plots.

In each of these stories you will find the spirit of jealousy raising its ugly head to destroy mankind. It seeks to destroy the men of God by accusation. Here it hopes to tarnish the *character and image* of God's followers. In order to overthrow you, the enemy needs to know your attributes; therefore, this spirit will use someone familiar or close to you. Also in these stories you will see the characters are given a specific name. They are called to serve God with all their heart, mind and soul; and they are commissioned to do a specific task. Let us call forth witnesses whose character was called into question; who showed extreme obedience and faith in God; and courage to stand up no matter what the cost. *Courage is a key element of the anointing granted to the believer at the last altar. Courage is a quality of being brave; the ability to face danger, difficulty, uncertainty or pain without being overcome by fear or being deflected from a chosen course of action; fearlessness, valor.* Only courage can allow you to perform regardless of fear. This anointing granted godly courage to Joshua and all the bible characters below. This courage is faith filled with passion which echoes a <u>nevertheless</u> praise. It states, do what you will with me; or to me but I can, I will, and I must stand for God. It gave one self control and security to venture in unfamiliar territory with the assurance that God would work on your behalf. Our God can do the same for you.

Below you will see many characters who knew the consequences to their actions were death, but they were committed to obey. Our first bible characters are the three Hebrew boys: Shadrach, Meshach and Abednego who served God, but were taken into captivity with Israel. They were given a choice to bow or die without any bargaining or compromise. Their Hebrew names were changed to Babylonian names containing to some reference of pagan gods. Here are the Hebrew and Babylonian name and their meaning. Hananiah meaning "Yahweh is gracious" was Shadrach: "aru, moon god; Mishael: "Who God is like?" was Meshach: "Who is as moon god"; and Azariah: "Yahweh is my helper"; was Abednego: "god of science and literature." These three men had pagan surroundings with new names, but they held fast to their Hebrew godly beliefs. In Daniel chapter three, the king made a decree, "That at what time ye hear the sound of the cornet, flute, harp, sackbut, psaltery, dulcimer, and all kinds of musick, ye fall down and worship the golden image that Nebuchadnezzar the king hath set up: And whosoever falleth not down and worshippeth shall the same hour be cast into the midst of a burning fiery furnace" (Daniel 3:5, 6). When Shadrach, Meshach and Abednego heard the sound, they would not bow down and worship the idol. They also told the king these words, "If it is so, our God whom we serve is able to deliver us from the burning fiery furnace, and he will deliver us out of thine hand, O king. But if not, (nevertheless) be it known unto thee, O king, that we will not serve thy gods, nor worship the golden image which thou hast set up (Daniel 3:17, 18). The statement outraged the king; so he commanded his servant to make the fire seven times hotter than normal. Then they were bound and thrown into the fire. The servants that threw them also were burned to death. An astonishing thing

Happened, three men were thrown into the fire; but, they saw four men. The conclusion to the matter was "He answered and said, Lo, I see four men loose, walking in the midst of the fire, and they have no hurt; and the form of the fourth is like the Son of God. The king made another decree that no one will speak against the God of Shadrach, Meshach, and Abednego and if so they shall be cut into pieces. He admitted there is a true and living powerful God who is greater than he. With great courage the Hebrews boys held to there faith and belief. God showed up mightily on the three Hebrews' behalf and declared his deity and glory.

Another character who shows extraordinary faith in God is Daniel. Daniel means, "God is my judge."

He had a spotless character, and the governors were jealous of his relationship with the king; so they wanted to trap him. They tricked the king to make a decree, "… that whoever petitions any god or man for thirty days, except you, O king, shall be cast into the den of lions" (Daniel 6:7 NKJV). He was determined to serve the true and living God. He refused to honor the decree. His punishment was to place him in the lions den. He was tested but God showed up on his behalf. God was gloried and his life was sustained because of his obedience and alignment to the will of God (Daniel 6).

Job is our next character; the meaning of his name is unknown. The Devil said Job was faithful to God only because He had blessed him. He detested that Job was blameless (without moral blemish) and upright (just, straightforward). The Devil asked God to remove the hedge from around Job. He claimed he would curse God and die. After the hedge was removed, he suffered many calamities at the hands of Satan; he lost his children and his property. Job immediately went to a place of worship (Job 1:20). He also lost his health, his wife's belief in him, and his friends' trust. Job stated, "Though He slay me, yet will I trust him" (Job 13:15).

Job continues to hold to divine insight. "But he knows the way that I take; When he has tested me, I shall come forth as gold" (Job 23:10). Job held onto God regardless of the pain, anxiety and distress. We all shall be tested and many times it won't make since naturally. It is clear the natural mind does not understand the happening at this altar. At this point Job seeks the wisdom of God to carry him through. So he declares: "But where, oh where, will they find Wisdom? Where does Insight hide? Mortals don't have a clue, haven't the slightest idea where to look. Earth's depths say, 'It's not here'; ocean deeps echo, 'Never heard of it.' It can't be bought with the finest gold; no amount of silver can get it. Even famous Ophir gold can't buy it, not even diamonds and sapphires. Neither gold nor emeralds are comparable; extravagant jewelry can't touch it. Pearl necklaces and ruby bracelets— why bother? None of this is even a down payment on Wisdom! Pile gold and African diamonds as high as you will, they can't hold to Wisdom. "So where does Wisdom come from? And where does Insight live? It can't be found by looking, no matter how deep you dig, no matter how high you fly. If you search through the graveyard and question the dead, they say,

'We've only heard rumors of it.' "God alone knows the way to Wisdom, he knows the exact place to find it. He knows where everything is on earth, he sees everything under heaven. After he commanded the winds to blow and measured out the waters, Arranged for the rain and set off explosions of thunder and lightning. He focused on Wisdom, made sure it was all set and tested and ready. Then he addressed the human race: 'Here it is! Fear-of-the-Lord—that's Wisdom, and Insight means shunning evil'" (Job 28:12-28, TM).

Job understood this wisdom and understanding could only be found in the spirit and man will never find it in the flesh. Both are needed to get through this test and trial.

Job friends felt he had done something wrong in order for this misfortunate to happen to him so they continuously slandered his character. In Job chapter 31 he declared his innocence and declared not guilty of: lust for women (v. 1-4), deceit and vanity (v. 5-6), or dishonesty (v. 7-8), or adultery (v. 9-12), or injustice (v. 13-15), or inhumanity (v. 16-23), or covetousness (v. 24-25), or idolatry (v. 26-28), or malignity (v. 29-31), or inhospitality (v. 32), or hypocrisy (v. 33-37), or fraud

(v. 38-40). Despite the criticism, discouragement, and condemnation; Job held to his faith and belief in God. He refused to bow, he refused to curse God and die. The enemy couldn't kill Job but he was hoping Job would get so depressed that he would kill himself. "...Also the Lord gave Job twice as much as he had before" (Job 42:10). Job held onto God until a powerful change came into his life. He understood this was a test; and after he was tried, it too would pass.

Not everyone escaped death. Stephen means "a crown." He was the first Christian martyred who held firmly to his position of faith. Stephen was selected by his brethren and appointed by the apostles to attend to the business affairs of the church. He had a good reputation and was full of the Holy Spirit and wisdom (Acts 6:3). Stephen was full of faith and power he did great wonders and signs among the people. Of course, there arose a jealous group who feared losing their influence and power with the people. They accused Stephen of speaking blasphemous words against the law (Acts 6:12), so they brought charges against him through false witnesses. The council held court and Stephen gave them a history lesson about the Law of Moses and

Israel. He told them of Israel's unfaithfulness and law-lessness. How they make much of the rite of physical circumcision authorized by Abraham. Finally, he stated, "You stiff-necked and uncircumcised in heart and ears! You always resist the Holy Spirit; as your fathers did, so do you. Which of the prophets did your fathers not persecute? And they killed those who foretold the coming of the Just One, of whom you now have become the betrayers and murderers, who have received the law by the direction of angels and have not kept it" (Acts 7:51-53 NKJV, WSB). He told them that the institutions and rituals of the law wouldn't get them into heaven without forgiveness from Jesus Christ. In the face of authorities, who were able to sentence him to death, Stephen <u>chose</u> to express the truth about Christ and the religious Jewish leaders of yesterday and today. His words were like a two-edge sword cutting hard and deep. He rebuked and left them with no argument so the crowd became violently angry at Stephen's words. These words were recorded about him, "When they heard these things they were cut to the heart, and they gnashed at him with their teeth. But he, being full of the Holy Spirit, gazed into heaven and saw the *glory of God,* (this is sum total of this altar) *and Jesus standing at the right hand of God, and said, "Look! I see the heavens opened and the Son of Man standing at the right hand of God!* Then they cried out with a loud voice, stopped their ears, and ran at him with one accord; and they cast him out of the city and stoned him" (Acts 7:54-58 NKJV). This is an account of God showing up (visitation) and showing himself mightily in the midst. This is the first time, ever recorded, where the ascended Lord is standing on the right hand of the Father, all others accounts he is sitting. He honors a layman filled with the spirit for his faith in Him. This vicious mob could not dispute the truth so they stoned Stephen to death.

Many women had great faith in God also. A courageous woman named Esther, whose faith was so strong in God that it saved her Jewish nation from death. The Queen Vashti disobeyed her husband. The King Ahasuerus wanted to show off his wife, Queen Vashti, to his drunken friends. He sent for her and she refused to come; so he dethroned her for disobeying him. He began looking for a new queen and Esther sought the position. Esther was a Jew who had been raised by her cousin, Mordecai. Esther's beauty captivated the king and she is chosen as queen. Now, Haman was second in command over this kingdom and despised Mordecai; for he refused to bow to him. So he plotted to have all the Jews killed; but Queen Esther was there escape. She vowed to go see the king whether she lived or died. The king favored Esther and granted her request to permit the Jews to live.

Deborah's strong faith delivered Barak and all Israel from the Canaanites. Rehab the harlot used her faith and helped the spies of Israel and her whole household was spared.

Here are the accounts and deliverance of God's followers; if He done it for them, He will do the same for you.

Conclusion: Relationship of Glory, change spirit or change soul.

1. Whole being unified.
2. Trust and dependency in God
3. God sends the answer.

4TH BAAL ALTAR DENUNCIATION OF GOD

PURPOSE: TO CAPTIVATE THE SOUL AND SENTENCE IT TO HELL!

This altar declares two things: lawlessness and the antichrist. These are two separate and distinct spirits. It is through this lawless heart and conscious, the deity of Christ is denounced, and the doctrines of devils are accepted. At this altar, the Spirit of Error heavily resists the Spirit of Truth. Lawlessness rejects and rebels against all biblical truths and doctrines. This spirit openly disobeys, rebels, and denies the Word of God.

Altar of

False Doctrines teaches against the principles of God.

Seared Consciousness; your mind, heart,

and spirit have been embodied by the Devil.

Anti Christ denies the Deity of Christ.

This altar seeks

1. Possession of the mind, body, and soul.

2. Condemning Power-the goal is to sentence

you to hell forever.

So let's see how we arrived at lawlessness. We begin with sin, which is an act, thought or way of behavior that goes against the law or teachings of God. This leads to disobedience, which is a refusal to obey. Next, it begets iniquity, a great injustice or extreme immorality that is a behavior. This advances into lawlessness, an uncontrollable or unregulated behavior; an outright deviancy and disobedience to the law. This lawlessness is continued iniquity which begun in the heart at the last altar. The bible defines lawlessness as iniquity and states below it is hidden. Since it's hidden, it is relatively deceptive. For the one who is deceived believes with all his

heart he is right, although he is wrong. If the Devil bla-
tantly came to deceive you, wouldn't you resist? Can
you see that deception is a key element of the Devil?
Throughout this book, deception is the first tool used.
This is the purpose of writing this book; so you will be
on guard for his tactics at the first altar. Please note that
you can fall into a state of non-repentance and rebellion,
which can become an irrevocable commitment that will
sentence you to hell.

In II Thessalonians chapter 2:3, Paul writes to assure
believers that Christ had not returned yet. He assured
them that the rapture was to happen first; afterwards,
apostasy and the antichrist would follow. He also told
them that he didn't send any letters written by false
teachers and he hadn't changed any laws or doctrines
previously written in the first epistle. He further stated:
*"Do you not remember that when I was still with you
I told you these things? And now you know what is
restraining, that he may be revealed in his own time.
For the mystery of lawlessness (iniquity) is already at
work; only He who now restrains will do so until He is
taken out of the way. And then the lawless one will be
revealed, whom the Lord will consume with the breath*

of His mouth and destroy with the brightness of His coming. The coming of the lawless one is according to the working of Satan, with all power, signs, and lying wonders, and with all unrighteous deception among those who perish, because they did not receive the love of the truth, that they might be saved. And for this reason God will send them strong delusion, that they should believe the lie, that they all may be condemned who did not believe the truth but had pleasure in unrighteousness (II Thess. 2:5-12 NKJV)." In addition, the things that are incited by the mystery of iniquity or lawlessness are found in I Timothy 4:1-2. *"Now the Spirit speaketh expressly, that in the latter times some shall depart from the faith, giving heed to seducing spirits, and doctrines of devils, speaking lies in hypocrisy; having their own conscience seared with a hot iron."* Here the writer is speaking of the latter day apostasy when many shall fall away and are drawn into evil by seducing spirits. All righteousness withers from the mind and it becomes cold, hardened and callous just like the heart. Deception has now hidden the truth from man and the choice to do what is right has withered away. Don't be fooled. If Satan could deceive and beguile one third of heaven's angels to rebel against God, what makes you feel that you can't be mislead. In the latter days, the very elect shall fall astray (Rev. 12:3-4).

During the Bush reign, our country found itself at war because of the misuse of power and lawlessness brought on by greed for oil. This administration deceived many of its leaders, along with the country. Many lives (at war) were lost because of the many lies told by the governmental system in order to receive power and monetary gain.

We saw this lawless spirit at work in the stock exchange and financial system when many citizens lost their life savings, jobs and homes in 2008 because they trusted our Government. They trusted it (the government) to make and follow laws that would insure the safety of the people. Due to lawlessness, our financial system crashed and we are now faced with a recession. Bernard Madoff stole 50 billion dollars from honest citizens in a money swindle because of lawlessness. Throughout life, men are always struggling to gain power, money and sex.

Therefore, this lawlessness progresses into rebellion. Rebellion is an organized attempt to overthrow a government or other authority by the use of force or violence. The key to this deceptive rule is, "do what thou wilt." This rule opposes the obedience to God and scripture. The Lord, said Himself, "...I do not seek My own will but the will of the Father who sent Me" (John 5:30 NKJV). When we defy God's authority and principles, we become rebellious. The Prophet Samuel states: For rebellion is as the sin of witchcraft. Some people are under its influence unknowingly. Rather you are under its influence by awareness or deceptive devices, the outcome is the same. Rebellion is the doorway for witchcraft. Witchcraft directly opens the door to the demonic realm. The goal of witchcraft is to control people or circumstances with or without their knowledge. In this deceptive principle, the person feels they are in control; but in actuality, they are in the process of becoming a slave to sin and corruption (II Peter 2:19). This step enables demonic bondage and oppression. We find witchcraft as one of the spirits at work in the first altar. It is the rebellion of many generations that hold family members hostage until the yokes are broken and destroyed.

God warned Cain of his disobedience with his sacrifice. He refused to repent and his choices determined his destiny. He chose to go his own way. His rebellious jealousy caused sin to control his choices and he killed his brother Abel (Gen. 4:1-8).

This open rebellion must lead to somewhere. Finally, we arrive at the state of apostasy; this is to renounce a religious faith, a set of principles, or a moral allegiance, a secession from the church, and a disowning of the name of Jesus and the power of His atoning blood. Paul states in Hebrews 3:12, *Take heed, brethren, lest there be in any of you an evil heart of unbelief, in departing from the living God. But exhort one another daily, while it is called Today; lest any of you be hardened through the deceitfulness of sin.* Here Paul is talking to the Christian (saved) not the unbeliever. He is warning them that the saved can return to an evil heart of unbelief, depart from the living God, be hardened by the deceitfulness of sin, be cut off like Israel, and finally lost in a state apostasy.

When a man reaches a state of apostasy, he believes, all faith in God and His redemptive work, is hopeless and nullified. He has no more faith, so all hope of repentance is gone. The seven stages of Apostasy can be found in Hebrews (NKJV) chapter three as Paul revisits Israel sinful ways:

1. Refusal to hear God and His Word (v. 7).

(7) Therefore, as the Holy Spirit says: "Today, if you will hear His voice."

2. Hardness of their heart by refusal to hear and obey God and His Word (v. 8, 13, 15).

(8) Do not harden your hearts as in the rebellion, In the day of trial in the wilderness. (13) but exhort one another daily while it is called "Today," lest you be hardened through the deceitfulness of sin. (15) while it is said: "Today, if you will hear His voice, Do not harden your hearts as in the rebellion."

3. Unbelief is a consequence of hardening the heart against God and His Word (v. 12)

4. Departure from the true and living God (v. 12).

(v12) Beware brethren, lest there be in any of you an evil heart of unbelief in departing from the living God;

5. Open rebellion against God and His Word to provoke anger and tempt Him (v. 8-9, 16).

(8-9) Do not harden your hearts as in the rebellion, In the day of trial in the wilderness, Where your fathers tested Me, tried Me, And saw My works forty years,

(16) For who, having heard, rebelled? Indeed, was it not all who came out of Egypt led by Moses?

6. Habitual sinning, careless and thoughtless living, and scandalous violation of God's laws (v. 10, 17).

(10) Therefore I was angry with that generation, And said, 'They always go astray in their heart, And they have not known My ways.' (17) Now with whom was He angry forty years? Was it not with those who sinned, whose corpses fell in the wilderness?

7. Finally apostasy (v. 11).

(11) So I swore in My wrath, "They shall not enter My rest."

It is here where a Christian can fully reject Jesus, his atoning work; so it is impossible for repentance and reconciliation to God. *"For it is impossible for those who were once enlightened, and have tasted of the heavenly gift, and were made partakers of the Holy Ghost, And have tasted the good word of God, and the powers of the world to come, If they shall fall away, to*

renew them again unto repentance; seeing they crucified to themselves the Son of God afresh, and put him
to an open shame. For the earth which drinketh in the
rain that cometh oft upon it, and bringeth forth herbs
meet for them by whom it is dressed, receiveth blessing
from God: But that which beareth thorns and briers is
rejected, and is nigh unto cursing; whose end is to be
burned." (Heb. 6:4-9).

Here below you will find the wickedness of man and
the characteristics of apostasy found in scripture: "But
know this, that in the last days perilous times will come:
For men will be lovers of themselves, lovers of money,
boasters, proud, blasphemers, disobedient to parents,
unthankful, unholy, unloving, unforgiving, slanderers,
without self-control, brutal, despisers of good, trai-
tors, headstrong, haughty, lovers of pleasure rather than
lovers of God (II Tim. 3:2-4 NKJV). Don't be fooled;
you can fall into apostasy right now.

In I Samuel 16:14 states, "But the Spirit of the Lord
departed from Saul, and an evil spirit from the Lord
troubled him". Saul continued to spiral downward and
became insanely jealous of David (I Sam. 18:8). He was

so enraged and embittered toward David, he tried to kill him three times (I Sam. 19:1, 10; 23:8). His rebellion caused him to fall, Saul finally turned to witchcraft, all because he refused to obey God (I Sam. 28:7). He went from the highest natural authority to the lowest camps of hell. When the downward cycle of sin starts, it continues; it is almost impossible to turn around. It takes the grace of our Lord and Savior Jesus Christ to turn us around. Saul's steps form a memory of selfish, egotism, pride, jealousy and abusive power. This led to moral and spiritual decay and lastly apostasy. Finally Saul was wounded in battle and killed himself by falling on his own sword (I Sam. 31:4; I Chron. 10). This act of suicide caused him to miss heaven.

Jude forewarned that the day would come when godless men would secretly infiltrate the ranks of the church. Who appeared to be pious, but beneath they are shameless scoundrels. Their purpose is to abuse and change the grace of God into a license for immorality. The ultimate end is to deny Jesus Christ our one and only Lord (Jude 1:4).

Jude states: But these people sneer at anything they can't understand, and by doing whatever they feel like doing—living by animal instinct only—they participate in their own destruction. I'm fed up with them! They're gone down Cain's road; they've been sucked into Balaam's error by greed; they've canceled out Korah's rebellion. These people are warts on your love feasts as you worship and eat together. They're giving you a black eye—carousing shamelessly, grabbing anything that isn't nailed down. They're—puffs of smoke pushed by gusts of wind; late autumn trees stripped clean of leaf and fruit, doubly dead, pulled up by the roots; wild ocean waves leaving nothing on the beach but the foam of their shame; Lost stars in outer space on their way to the black hole.

Enoch, the seventh after Adam, prophesied of this: "Look! The Master comes with thousands of holy angels to bring judgment against them all, convicting each person of every defiling act of shameless sacrilege, of every dirty word they have spewed of their pious filth." These are the "grumpers," the bellyachers, grabbing for the biggest piece of pie, talking big, saying anything they think will get them ahead.

But remember dear friends, that the apostles of our Master Jesus Christ, told us this would happen: "In the last days there will be people who don't take these things seriously anymore. They'll treat them like a joke, and make a religion of their own whims and lusts." They are the ones who split churches, thinking only of themselves. There's nothing to them, no sign of the spirit! (Jude 1:10-23 TMB)

Little children, it is the last hour; and as you have heard that the <u>Antichrist is coming</u>, even now <u>many antichrists have come</u>, by which we know that it is the last hour. They went out from us, but they were not of us; for if they had been of us, they would have continued with us; but they went out that they might be manifest, that none of them were of us. But you have an anointing from the Holy One, and you know all things. I have not written to you because you do not know the truth, but because you know it, and that no lie is of the truth. Who is a liar but he who denies that Jesus is the Christ? He is antichrist who denies the Father and the Son. Whoever denies the Son does not have the Father either; he who acknowledges the Son has the Father also (I John 2:18-23). So let's see what the meaning of antichrist is. Christ is Christos, in the Greek which is equal to the word Mashiach, in the Hebrew, which means Messiah. When we say antichrist we are actually saying anti-Messiah. The Devil's plan is to put a false messenger in the place of the true Messiah. By this, you know the Spirit of God: Every spirit that confesses that Jesus Christ {the Messiah} has come in the flesh is of God, and every spirit that does not confess that Jesus {the Messiah} has come in the flesh is not of God. And this is the spirit of the Antichrist, which you have heard was coming, and is now already in the world (I John 4:2-3 NKJV, WSB). In these passages, we see three different types of antichrist. First, listed is the Antichrist, the person, who is coming to deceive the world (we will discuss him later). Second, there are the many antichrists, which will come in the form of false prophets and teachers, etc. Verse 19 gives us to know they will be among God's people. It also denies that Christ is the Messiah and denies the Father and the Son (v. 22). Last, they deny that the Messiah has come already. Third, the spirit of the antichrist which is the rebellious spirit that operates through the antichrist. He is a man of lawlessness.

These false prophets and teachers will arise teaching heresies and devoting themselves to desecration. They are Satan's messengers and ambassadors who come to deceive, delude and destroy the precious souls of men. The false prophet seeks to convert men to themselves for material gain and power. They are character destroyers instead of builders. Their goal is to cause separation between God and man. He comes to pluck righteousness out the heart and fill it with rebellious iniquity. The false prophets will destroy man's moral concepts and behaviors. The false prophet is not just a New Testament phenomenal, but has distorted God's view for ages, as in the Old Testament era. This is Peter's viewpoint of the false prophet: But there were also lying prophets among the people then, just as there will be lying religious teachers among you. They'll smuggle in destructive divisions, pitting you against each other—biting the hand of the One who gave them a chance to have their lives back! They've put themselves on a fast downhill slide to destruction, but not before they recruit a crowd of mixed-up followers who can't tell right from wrong (II Pet 2:1-2 TMB).

They've left the main road and are directionless, having taken the way of Balaam, son of Beor, the prophet who turned profiteer, a connoisseur of evil... There's nothing to these people—they're dried-up fountains, storm-scattered clouds, headed for a black hole in hell. They are loudmouths, full of hot air, but still they're dangerous. Men and women who have recently escaped from a deviant life are most susceptible to their brand of seduction. They promise these newcomers freedom, but they themselves are slaves of corruption, for if they're addicted to corruption—and they are—they're enslaved (II Pet. 2:17-19 TMB). Don't be deceived, the false prophet is a religious imposter; a master counterfeiter; a propagator of false doctrine. *But evil men and impostors will grow worse and worse, deceiving and being deceived (*II Tim. 3:13 NKJV).

Matthew 7:15-23 NIV states, "Watch out for false prophets. They come to you in sheep's clothing, but inwardly they are ferocious wolves. By their fruit you will recognize them. Do people pick grapes from thornbushes, or figs from thistles? Likewise every good tree bears good fruit, but a bad tree bears bad fruit. A good tree cannot bear bad fruit, and a bad tree cannot bear good fruit. Every tree that does not bear good fruit is cut down and thrown into the fire. Thus by their fruit you will recognize them."

"Not everyone who says to me, 'Lord, Lord,' will enter the kingdom of heaven, but only he who does the will of my Father who is in heaven. Many will say to me on that day, 'Lord, Lord, did we not prophesy in your name, and in your name drive out demons and perform many miracles?" Then I will tell them plainly, 'I never knew you. Away from me, you evildoers!'

And Jesus answered and said to them, "Take heed that no one deceives you. For many will come in My name, saying, I am the Christ, and will deceive many… Then if anyone says to you, 'Look, here is the Christ!' or 'There!' do not believe it. For false christs and false prophets will rise and show great signs and wonders to deceive, if possible, even the elect. See, I have told you beforehand" (Matt. 24:4-5; 23-25 NKJV).

Below are some identifying behaviors of the false prophet: The false prophet opposes the will and plans of God? He seeks to glory in his own power and authority.

He is determined to do his own thing, no matter what the cost. The false prophet will reject truth and rob man of his spiritual and eternal life. His thought process is warped with total deception. He is controlled by the deceptive father of all lies and the mastermind of all delusions, the Devil. He is a fraud and the perpetrator of godliness. His outer appearance will seem godly, but his inside is evil and corrupt. These false prophets are liken to the Pharisees found in Matt 23:25-28 TMB: "You're hopeless, you religion scholars and Pharisees! Frauds! You burnish the surface of your cups and bowls so they sparkle in the sun, while the insides are maggoty with your greed and gluttony. Stupid Pharisee! Scour the insides, and then the gleaming surface will mean something. You're hopeless, you religion scholars and Pharisees! Frauds! You're like manicured grave plots, grass clipped and the flowers bright, but six feet down its all rotting bones and worm-eaten flesh. People look at you and think you're saints, but beneath the skin you're total frauds."

They are men pleasers, instead of God lovers. They are skillful orators who speak things of splendor and flattery. They seek to entertain with folly and foolishness.

They twist the truth to fit and suit their circumstances. They fill the spirit with mischief, and poison the heart with evil. In the book of Isaiah, the prophets listened to rebellious Israel: They say to the seers, "See no more visions!" and to the prophets, "Give us no more visions of what is right! Tell us pleasant things, prophesy illusions. Leave this way, get off this path, and stop confronting us with the Holy One of Israel!" (Isaiah 30:10-11 NIV). The prophet's were to seek God for His vision and word, but they disobeyed and gave into the people's evil ways. They handle holy things without fear and reverence. Jeremiah stated, "A horrible and shocking thing has happened in the land: The prophets prophesy lies, the priests rule by their own authority, and my people love it this way. But what will you do in the end? (Jeremiah 5:30-31 NIV).

These false prophets are doomed and hell bound and their message must be rejected (Jer. 23:15-18). If not, you too are hell bound. God didn't let the rebel angels off the hook, but jailed them in hell till Judgment Day. Neither did he let the ancient ungodly world off. He wiped it out with a flood, rescuing only eight people— Noah, the sole voice of righteousness, was one of the them. God decreed destruction for the cities of Sodom and Gomorrah. A mound of ashes was all that was left— as a grim warning to anyone bent on an ungodly life. But that good man Lot, driven nearly out of his mind by the sexual filth and perversity, was rescued. Surrounded by moral rot day after day, that righteous man was in constant torment. So God knows how to rescue the godly from evil trials. And he knows how to hold the feet of the wicked to the fire until Judgment Day (II Pet. 2:4-9 TMB).

The false prophet message is filled with false visions, divinations and deceit. It will root and ground converts into hypocrisy and lies. The message does not challenge or reprove the Christian lifestyle of holiness and righteous ethics. The Lord said he never spoke to them nor commanded them to speak (Jer. 14:14). They speak the worthless message of their own evil heart. In the Message Bible, the prophet Jeremiah speaks harshly about the false prophet; for they prophesied by Baal and led God's people astray. He declares in Jeremiah 23:9-40 TMB:

The "Everything Will Turn Out Fine" Sermon

My head is reeling, my limbs are limp, I'm staggering like a drunk, seeing double from too much wine—And all because of God, because of his holy words. Now for what God says regarding the lying prophets: "Can you believe it? A country teeming with adulterers! faithless, promiscuous idolater-adulterers! They're a curse on the land. The land's a wasteland. Their unfaithfulness is turning the country into a cesspool, Prophets and priests devoted to desecration. They have nothing to do with me as their God. My very own Temple, mind you— mud-spatter with their crimes." God's Decree. "But they won't get by with it. They'll find themselves on a slip- pery slope, careening into the darkness, somersaulting into the pitch-black dark. I'll make them pay for their crimes. It will be the Year of Doom." God's Decree.

"Over in Samaria I saw prophets acting like silly fools—shocking! They preached using that no-god Baal for a text, messing with the minds of my people. And the Jerusalem prophets are even worse—horrible!—sex driven, living a lie, subsidizing a culture of wickedness, and never giving it a second thought. They're as bad as those wretches in old Sodom, the degenerates of old Gomorrah." So here's the Message to the prophets from

God-of-the-Angel-Armies: "I'll cook them a supper of maggoty meat with after-dinner drinks of strychnine. The Jerusalem prophets are behind all this. They're the cause of the godlessness polluting the country." A Message from the God-of-the-Angel-Armies: "Don't listen to the sermons of the prophets. It's all hot air. Lies, lies, and more lies. They make it all up. Not a word they speak comes from me. They preach their 'Everything Will Turn Out Fine' sermon to the congregations with no taste for God, Their 'Nothing Bad Will Turn Ever Happen To You' sermon to people who are set in their own ways. "Have any of these prophets bothered to meet with me, the true God? bothered to take in what I have to say? Listened to and then lived out my Word? Look out! God's hurricane will be let loose—my hurricane blast, Spinning the heads of the wicked like tops! God's raging anger won't let up until I've made a clean sweep, completing the job I began. When the job's done, you'll see that it's been well done.

Quit The "God Told Me This" Kind of Talk

"I never sent these prophets, but they ran anyway. I never spoke to them, but they preached away. If they'd have bothered to sit down and meet with me, they'd have preached my Message to my people. They'd have gotten them back on the right track, gotten them out of their evil ruts.

"Am I not a God near at hand"—God's Decree—"and not a God a far off? Can anyone hide out in a corner where I can't see him? God's Decree. "Am I not present everywhere, whether seen or unseen?" God's Decree.

I know what they're saying, all these prophets who preach lies using me as their text, saying "I had this dream! I had this dream! How long do I have to put up with this? Do these prophets give two cents about me as they preach their lies and spew out their grandiose delusions? They swap dreams one with another, feed on each other's delusive dreams, trying to distract my people from me just as their ancestors were distracted by the no-god Baal.

"You prophets who do nothing but dream—go ahead and tell your silly dreams. But you prophets who have a message from me—tell it truly faithfully. What does straw have in common with wheat? Nothing else is like God's Decree. Isn't my Message like fire?" God's Decree. "Isn't it like a sledgehammer busting a rock?

"I've had it I've with the 'prophets' who get all their sermons secondhand from each other. Yes, I've had it with them. They make up stuff and then pretend it's a real sermon.

"Oh yes, I've had it with the prophets who preach the lies they dream up, spreading them all over the country, ruining the lives of my people with their cheap and reckless lies.

"I never sent these prophets, never authorized a single one of them. They do nothing for this people — nothing!" God's Decree.

"And anyone, including prophets and priests, who asks, 'What's God got to say about all this, what's troubling him? tell him, 'You, you're the trouble, and I'm getting rid of you.'" God's Decree.

"And if anyone, including prophets and priests, goes around saying glibly 'God's Message! God's Message!' I'll punish him and his family.

"Instead of claiming to know what God says, ask questions of one another, such as 'How do we understand God in this?' But don't go around pretending to know it all, saying 'God told me this...'God told me that...' I don't want to hear it anymore. Only the person I authorize speaks for me. Otherwise, my Message gets twisted, the Message of the living God-of-the-Angel-Armies.

"You can ask the prophets, 'How did God answer you? What did he tell you?' But don't pretend that you know all the answers yourselves and talk like you know it all. I'm telling you: Quit the 'God told me this...God told me that...kind of talk'.

"Are you paying attention? You'd better, because I'm about to take you in hand and throw you to the ground, you and this entire city that I gave to your ancestors. I've had it with the lot of you. You're never going to live this down. You're going down in history as a disgrace."

These false prophets are constantly seeking ways to enlarge their own territories and purses. They gather men unto themselves for their own selfish motives. "They'll say anything, that sounds good to exploit" their followers of all there earthly and heavenly possessions (II Pet. 2:3 TMB). They build earthly kingdoms that will perish and fade away. *Frauds!* "I've had it with you! You're hopeless, you religion scholars, you Pharisees! Frauds! Your lives are roadblocks to God's kingdom. You refuse to enter, and won't let anyone else in either. You're hopeless, you religion scholars and Pharisees!

Frauds! You go halfway around the world to make a convert, but once you get him you make him into a replica of yourselves, double-damned" (Matt. 23:15 TMB).

They prey on the weak. These people are nothing but brute, beasts, born in the wild, predators on the prowl. In the very act of bringing down others with their ignorant blasphemies, they themselves will be brought down, losers in the end. Their evil will boomerang on them. They're so despicable and addicted to pleasure that they indulge in wild parties, carousing in broad daylight. They're obsessed with adultery, compulsive sin, seducing every vulnerable soul they come upon. Their specialty is greed. And they're experts at it. Dead souls! (II Pet. 2:12-16 TMB).

In Micah 3:1-7 the Lord said the prophets "*make my people error.*" They draw them into wickedness and falsehood. They taught them to hate good and love evil. These false prophets and teachers shall rise deceiving entire households. It is here men will consecrate themselves to false doctrines and unsound faith, serving divers lusts and pleasures (Titus 1:10-16).

"For the time will come when they will not endure sound doctrine, but according to their own desires, because they have itching ears, they will heap up for themselves teachers; and they will turn their ears away from the truth, and be turned aside to fables." (II Timothy 4:3-4 NKJV). It is an end time apostasy. It is here that the deceptive false prophet will arise, another man who is a religious leader of the antichrist. He is an evil miracle worker showing forth signs and wonders of supernatural powers. He will bring down fire from heaven and have the people (of the tribulation period) to make an "image of the beast" so they may worship it. He will have power to bring life to this image and cause it to speak and demand all that will not worship the anti-christ be put to death (Rev. 13:14-15). He will cause all in the kingdom of the antichrist to be branded with the name or mark (666) placed in their right hand or in their foreheads. There will be a law that no one, without the mark, can buy or sell anything. He will be taken at the same time with the antichrist at Armageddon and be cast into the lake of fire (Rev. 13:11-18; 19:20; 20:10).

The Antichrist is the final manifestation of the spirit of antichrist and the Devil's last stance. *Let no one deceive you by any means, for that Day will not come (the coming of the Lord) unless the falling away comes first, and the man of sin is revealed, the son of perdition* (II Thess. 2:3). Falling away in the Greek is apostacia meaning an apostasy, which is a deliberate rebellion and rejection of God and the revealed truth. The Antichrist is the supreme embodiment of lawlessness and the leader of the great apostasy. He will be called the "man of sin" (II Thess. 4:3, 8-12; Rev. 13:1; 14:9-13; 15:2-4; 16:2-12). The antichrist is called the "son of perdition", for his destiny is destruction because of his rebellion. He also will sell himself to Satan just as Judas (II Thess. 4:3, 8-12; John. 17:12; Dan. 8:24; 11:37-39). In Revelation 13:1-4: *I saw a beast rising up out of the sea, having seven heads and ten horns, and on his horns ten crowns, and on his heads a blasphemous name. Now the beast which I saw was like a leopard, his feet were like the feet of a bear, and his mouth like the mouth of a lion. The dragon gave him his power, his throne, and great authority. And I saw one of his heads as if it had been mortally wounded, and his deadly wound was healed. And all the world marveled and followed the beast. So they worshipped the dragon who gave authority to the beast; and they worshipped the beast, saying, "Who is*

like the beast? Who is able to make war with him?"
Here the Antichrist is also known as "the beast" a person
to whom Satan will give his power. Satan will give him
his power so the beast (Antichrist) can gain power over
humanity. His goal is for the beast to persuade humanity
to worship Satan. He has been working and waiting for
this many centuries.

He has a specific time to be revealed, and he is an
opposer of Christ. He will exalt himself above God and
will not deny being worshipped as God. The spirit of
lawlessness cannot be revealed until the hinderer of lawlessness (the church) is removed from the world. When
this wicked one is revealed, he will live until the second
advent of Christ. The wicked one will head the armies at
Armageddon and will be doomed and destroyed (killed)
by Christ (v. 8; Dan 7:24-2, 8:23-27, 9:27, 11:36-45;
12:1-7; Rev. 19:11-21; Mt. 24:15-31).

He is a man, and a deceiver (v. 10; Dan. 8:24-25;
9:27; 11:36-45; Mt. 24:15-32; Rev. 13:1-18; 19: 20), in
whom Satan will dwell utterly and boldly, he will have
satanic and demonic miraculous powers (v. 9; Dan.
8:24; 11: 37-39; Rev. 13:2, 11-18; 16: 13-16; 19:20; Mt.
24:24). Only those who love sin, reject the truth of God

and refuse salvation shall be deceived by him (v. 11-12). He will come with great delusions and a lie (v. 11-12; Dan. 8:10-14, 25; 11:39).

In the Old Testament he is prefigured under "king of Babylon" (Isa. 14:4); the little "horn" (Dan. 7:8, 8 :9); the king "insolent and skilled in intrigue" (8:23); "the prince who is to come" (9:26); the willful king (11:36).

In the New Testament he is called "the man of law-lessness," the son of destruction" (II Thess. 2:3-8), "antichrist" (I John 2:18); and the beast" (Rev. 13:1-10). This sinister, demon-inspired leader will rise to dominate the world in the end-time, persecute the saints, seek to destroy the Jewish nation, and banish the name of God and Christ from the earth, and thus take over. This would mean the thwarting of God's plan for the messianic millennial kingdom, which involves the restoration of Israel (Acts 1:6) and universal peace.

He is destroyed by the second advent of Christ (Rev. 19:11-16), who sets up the earthly kingdom (Rev. 20:13).

Conclusion: Relationship of Death

    1. Declares lawlessness.

    2. Believes in the anti-Christ.

    3. The soul is condemned to hell.

About the Author

S hirley Nash recognized at an early aged she had a prophetical calling upon her life. She is a saved woman of virtue and wisdom. She has a phenomenal teaching/counseling ministry that has transformed lives forever. She has taught at many conferences and seminars for men and women. She teaches yearly at Blue Ridge Mountains for various groups.

Shirley was the first female in the Eastern Jurisdiction COGIC to score 100 on the Evangelist Test. She attended Deliverance Bible Institute and Gary Whetstone Bible Institute.

She co-founded New Covenant Ministries with her husband Elder Reginald Nash.

She received a degree from Community College of Philadelphia in Mental Health Social Science achieving first honors, upon which she was inducted into the Phi Beta Kappa Honors Society. She worked as a Drug and Alcohol Therapist sharing a new vision and new hope for many weary souls. She also was a rape counselor with (WAR) Woman Against Rape.

Above all she is a wonderful wife, a dedicated mother, a loving grandmother, and a very giving foster mother.

CPSIA information can be obtained
at www.ICGtesting.com
Printed in the USA
BVHW03s1143290818
525947BV00001B/8/P